JUMPSTART CRIMINAL LAW

Reading and Understanding Criminal Law Cases and Statutes

JUMPSTART CRIMINAL LAW

Reading and Understanding Criminal Law Cases and Statutes

JOHN M. BURKOFF

Professor of Law
University of Pittsburgh School of Law

ROSS SANDLER

Professor of Law
New York Law School
Jumpstart Series Editor

Wolters Kluwer
Law & Business

Published by Wolters Kluwer Law & Business in New York.

Wolters Kluwer Law & Business serves customers worldwide with CCH, Aspen Publishers, and Kluwer Law International products (www.wolterskluwerlb.com).

To contact Customer Service, e-mail customer.service@wolterskluwer.com, call 1-800-234-1660, fax 1-800-901-9075, or mail correspondence to:

Wolters Kluwer Law & Business
Attn: Order Department
PO Box 990
Frederick, MD 21705

Printed in the United States of America.

1 2 3 4 5 6 7 8 9 0

ISBN 978-1-4548-2379-7

Library of Congress Cataloging-in-Publication Data

Burkoff, John M.
    Jumpstart criminal law : reading and understanding criminal law cases and statutes / John M. Burkoff, Professor of Law, University of Pittsburgh School of Law.
        pages cm
    Includes index.
    ISBN 978-1-4548-2379-7 (alk. paper)
    1. Criminal law—United States. I. Title.
    KF9219.85.B874 2013
    345.73—dc23

                                                                      2013002276

About Wolters Kluwer Law & Business

Wolters Kluwer Law & Business is a leading global provider of intelligent information and digital solutions for legal and business professionals in key specialty areas, and respected educational resources for professors and law students. Wolters Kluwer Law & Business connects legal and business professionals as well as those in the education market with timely, specialized authoritative content and information-enabled solutions to support success through productivity, accuracy and mobility.

Serving customers worldwide, Wolters Kluwer Law & Business products include those under the Aspen Publishers, CCH, Kluwer Law International, Loislaw, Best Case, ftwilliam.com and MediRegs family of products.

CCH products have been a trusted resource since 1913, and are highly regarded resources for legal, securities, antitrust and trade regulation, government contracting, banking, pension, payroll, employment and labor, and healthcare reimbursement and compliance professionals.

Aspen Publishers products provide essential information to attorneys, business professionals and law students. Written by preeminent authorities, the product line offers analytical and practical information in a range of specialty practice areas from securities law and intellectual property to mergers and acquisitions and pension/benefits. Aspen's trusted legal education resources provide professors and students with high-quality, up-to-date and effective resources for successful instruction and study in all areas of the law.

Kluwer Law International products provide the global business community with reliable international legal information in English. Legal practitioners, corporate counsel and business executives around the world rely on Kluwer Law journals, looseleafs, books, and electronic products for comprehensive information in many areas of international legal practice.

Loislaw is a comprehensive online legal research product providing legal content to law firm practitioners of various specializations. Loislaw provides attorneys with the ability to quickly and efficiently find the necessary legal information they need, when and where they need it, by facilitating access to primary law as well as state-specific law, records, forms and treatises.

Best Case Solutions is the leading bankruptcy software product to the bankruptcy industry. It provides software and workflow tools to flawlessly streamline petition preparation and the electronic filing process, while timely incorporating ever-changing court requirements.

ftwilliam.com offers employee benefits professionals the highest quality plan documents (retirement, welfare and non-qualified) and government forms (5500/PBGC, 1099 and IRS) software at highly competitive prices.

MediRegs products provide integrated health care compliance content and software solutions for professionals in healthcare, higher education and life sciences, including professionals in accounting, law and consulting.

Wolters Kluwer Law & Business, a division of Wolters Kluwer, is headquartered in New York. Wolters Kluwer is a market-leading global information services company focused on professionals.

Dedicated with love to Nancy, Amy & Sean,
David & Emmy, Emma, Molly, Hannah, and Cyrus.

Contents

CHAPTER 4

Context: Steps in the Criminal Justice Process

CHAPTER 5

Criminal Trials: Judge and Jury

Statutory Element Analysis: The Way Criminal Law Works

Criminal Defenses: Three Distinct Types

Preface

The primary purpose of this concise *Jumpstart Criminal Law* book is to give students in Criminal Law courses the background and contextual material they need to help them be successful in that course, and to have a better handle on the material—cases and statutes—that is being studied. A secondary purpose of *Jumpstart Criminal Law*, however, is simply to demystify this subject matter. To that end, you don't need to be taking a Criminal Law course to learn something very important from *Jumpstart Criminal Law* about the nature of criminal prosecutions, criminal defense, and criminal trials in United States courts.

Law students are directed to read and analyze judicial opinions in Criminal Law courses, focusing in particular upon those courts' application of statutory language in determining whether or not a crime has been committed. But learning Criminal Law, simply by reading judicial opinions and statutes, challenges even the most capable and conscientious first-year law students. *Jumpstart Criminal Law* helps to make this study of Criminal Law less confusing; it offers you an introductory road map through what is otherwise often-treacherous intellectual terrain.

What kind of road map does this book offer you? Hmmm. In the age of ubiquitous GPS devices, do you even know what a "road map" is? What do I mean when I say that? Well, let me answer that by telling you what background and contextual material *Jumpstart Criminal Law* actually covers.

Chapter 1 starts you off by explaining what the study of Criminal Law includes in the United States and, just as important, what it does not include. Chapter 3 introduces you to some of the most important contextual points, focusing upon the key concepts of jurisdictional variance in United States Criminal Law, and the relationship between state and federal Criminal Law statutes.

Chapter 4 is particularly useful to students—or, frankly, to anyone—new to this area, detailing the steps (in chronological order) that take place in the criminal justice process, from the investigation or report of a crime to the appeal of a conviction. In that same explanatory vein, Chapter 2 defines for you the language of the law, and more specifically, the language of the Criminal Law (often called "terms of art"). What are judges, prosecutors, and defense counsel talking about? What do they mean when they use standard English in what seems, to the lay listener at least, a novel way? Chapter 4 gives you the low down.

Chapter 5 explains the differing roles of the criminal trial judge and the jury in United States criminal trials. Understanding the fundamental points introduced here makes the analysis of decisional law in criminal cases much easier, and more sensible.

Chapter 6 discusses the focal approach to the prosecution and defense of criminal cases in the United States—so-called "element analysis." Understand this basic Criminal Law method of analysis, and you can better understand what judges are saying—and why they are saying it—in the decisions you read in class. And usefully, this method of analysis also enables you to better understand why criminal cases you hear discussed in the media have been decided the way they have. Chapter 7 continues with this theme, centering more specifically on the nature and significance of the different types of Criminal Law defenses.

Chapter 8 introduces you to the topic of why and how particular conduct is criminalized (or not criminalized). To truly understand how the Criminal Law "works," you need to know what is actually punished, how it came to be punished, and the political significance of that process of criminalization. This process is not pretty, and it may not work the way you thought or wished that it did. But, like it or not, it is important for you to know how this process works in any event. Chapter 10 focuses more specifically on two of the most important concepts in United States Criminal Law: mens rea and actus reus. What do these terms of art mean? Chapter 10 lays it out for you.

Chapter 9 provides you with the most effective analytic tool for assessing and understanding the Criminal Law decisions you will be discussing in a Criminal Law class, mostly decisions handed down by appellate judges. Why focus on appellate decisions? Well, Chapter 11 answers that question, discussing the significance of the study of appellate court—rather than trial court—decisions.

Chapter 12 takes a more pragmatic view of success in a Criminal Law course, giving you specific pointers on how to be successful on the standard sorts of Criminal Law exams. And, finally, Chapter 13 tries to sum up what you should have learned from all of these chapters in *Jumpstart Criminal Law*, offering some concluding thoughts.

The heavily edited brief extracts from judicial opinions included in *Jumpstart Criminal Law* are intended to complement the substantive material that is covered in any of the many Criminal Law casebooks used in law schools across the United States (including mine). What *Jumpstart Criminal Law* adds to that coverage is, once again, a road map. Follow that road map and you are bound to be more successful in your Criminal Law course, and hopefully, you will also be better situated to master some of the skills you need to become an effective and successful lawyer.

John M. Burkoff
February 2013

JUMPSTART CRIMINAL LAW

Reading and Understanding Criminal Law Cases and Statutes

CHAPTER 1

What Can You Learn from *Jumpstart Criminal Law*?

A. INTRODUCTION

Jumpstart Criminal Law is intended to give you an informed context for the study of U.S. Criminal Law.

The subject of Criminal Law is all about criminal offenses and defenses, guilt and innocence, and prosecution and defense. *But* . . . all of these things take place in a larger—a much larger—setting. You'll learn more—and you'll understand more—about the substantive Criminal Law doctrine you will study in a Criminal Law course when you have *first* had the chance to learn about and to appreciate the context in which criminal statutes are drafted and enacted and in which criminal trials and appeals take place.

What do I mean here by talking about the "context" and "setting" of Criminal Law?

The best way to answer that question is to give you some examples. Here are just a few of the stage-setting, contextual matters that are discussed in this *Jumpstart Criminal Law* book:

- The relationship between state and federal criminal prosecutions and trials;
- the difference between criminal offenses and defenses in different U.S. jurisdictions;
- the steps in the criminal justice process (what happens when . . . and why?);
- the meaning of the criminal justice system's "terms of art";
- the separate roles of judge and jury in criminal cases and their significance;
- "element analysis" in criminal cases and with criminal statutes;
- the nature of the different types of Criminal Law defenses;
- criminal defense ethics (not an oxymoron);

- how, when, and why conduct is criminalized; and
- the role of "mens rea" and "actus reus" in Criminal Law.

Moreover, the study of Criminal Law is easier—and, hopefully, makes much more sense—when you have begun it by focusing upon some special analytical skills useful for that field of study.

Like what?

Well, once again, let me explain by giving you just a few examples of the special analytical skills that are discussed in this *Jumpstart Criminal Law* book:

- *Understanding* how to distinguish Criminal Law from Torts;
- *applying* "element analysis";
- *learning* the basic lines of defense against criminal charges;
- *figuring out* how to analyze appellate decisions; and
- *preparing* for Criminal Law exams.

B. IT'S NOT CRIMINAL PROCEDURE OR CRIMINAL PROCESS

One of the things that you need to understand early on is just what Criminal Law *is*. It's about, as previously mentioned: the elements of (substantive) criminal offenses and defenses, proof of guilt and innocence, and the requirements and skills of prosecution and defense.

It's also important to know what Criminal Law *is not*. It's *not* Criminal Procedure, for example. The term "Criminal Procedure" is something of a misnomer, by the way. If you've already taken or are taking a course in Civil Procedure, you might naturally think that Criminal Procedure is the study of the procedural rules relating to litigation in U.S. courts. That would make sense, of course. But that's not what Criminal Procedure is really about for the most part (although similar procedural rules do exist).

A Criminal Procedure course focuses on the rights of individuals as against the State when they are being investigated and the rights of the accused when they are being prosecuted. At many law schools, these two subtopics are taught in two separate Criminal Procedure courses.

In the United States, unlike many other countries, the Criminal Procedure course focuses on the U.S. Constitution, primarily portions of the Bill of Rights and the Fourteenth Amendment; i.e., *it's a "con law" course*. It's also a human rights course. In fact, at your school, the course may well be called "*Constitutional Criminal Procedure*," which is a much more accurate description of the course content.

The Bill of Rights is comprised of the first 10 amendments to the U.S. Constitution, which were all adopted in 1791. The Fourteenth Amendment was subsequently adopted in 1868, after—and as a direct result of—the end of the Civil War. The portions of those amendments relevant to rights in the criminal justice system are these:

- The **Fourth Amendment's** right against "unreasonable searches and seizures" and "Warrant Clause";
- the **Fifth Amendment's** "Grand Jury Clause," "Double Jeopardy Clause," "Self-Incrimination Clause," and "Due Process Clause";
- the **Sixth Amendment's** right to a speedy trial, right to a public trial, right to a jury, right to be informed of the nature of the charges filed against the accused, "Confrontation Clause," "Compulsory Process Clause," and right to counsel;
- the **Eighth Amendment's** "Excessive Bail Clause," "Excessive Fines Clause," and "Cruel and Unusual Punishment Clause"; and
- the **Fourteenth Amendment's** "Due Process Clause" and "Equal Protection Clause."

As noted, these Bill of Rights provisions are *not* (usually) discussed as a regular part of a *Criminal Law* course; they contain material about individual rights that is covered in-depth in *Criminal Procedure* courses. *But* . . . some of the content of those constitutional provisions is most definitely a part of the context in which criminal prosecutions take place. Hence, it is an important part of the *context* of Criminal Law.

So, hey, lucky you! You don't have to wait for a Criminal Procedure course to learn more about some of the most important aspects of this Bill of Rights content. We'll discuss it here . . . in *Jumpstart Criminal Law*.

C. IT'S NOT TORTS

There's another important legal subject you need to recognize that Criminal Law is *not*—that's Torts!

Actually, the reason for some of the similarity between these two bodies of law is this: *Criminal Law grew out of the law of torts.* Until the Fourteenth Century in England, there was no separate body of Criminal Law. There were only torts, civil wrongs. *See* Chapter 8 on the development of common law crimes. Torts were—and are—of course, *private* wrongs, actionable by private parties. Litigants seek to recover compensation from alleged tort-feasors for the damages caused by their tortious conduct.

Criminal offenses, in contrast, are *public* wrongs and involve proceedings brought against individuals (usually) by the State. The State is not seeking economic redress for the actions of the accused; it is seeking *to punish* the accused for his or her antisocial and harmful conduct.

Of course, the same conduct committed by the same individual can be a crime . . . *and a tort.*

For example, if X runs over and kills Y one rainy night when X is driving too fast for the weather conditions, X may be guilty of a crime (such as reckless driving or vehicular homicide) *and* a tort (such as wrongful death). The criminal case would be prosecuted in the *criminal* courts, and the civil torts case would be prosecuted in the *civil* courts.

Indeed, X might be acquitted of a crime and still have a judgment entered against him in the civil case, even though they both arise out of the identical facts. This is particularly true because the burden of proof is usually quite different in the two venues, civil and criminal: Crimes need to be established beyond a reasonable doubt (*see* Chapter 5); torts can be established at trial (usually) by a lesser showing of a preponderance of the evidence.

One of the reasons that you need to remain cognizant that these are two separate bodies of law is that they often discuss principles that sound as if they are the same. But while they may sound similar, they are not the same. This is particularly true of two areas—the law relating to negligence and the law relating to causation.

Both a Criminal Law course and a Torts course generally involve detailed discussion of the application of negligence principles and the concept of causation. But in most jurisdictions, the law relating to these two subjects in these two different venues is different. The key difference, typically, is that it is more difficult to establish negligence and causation in the criminal setting than it is in the civil setting.

CASE 1. Drag racing death on the highway: Criminal Law principles are not usually the same as Tort principles, even where some of the terminology is the same; e.g., "causation." *So be careful!*

THE DRAG RACE ON THE COUNTRY ROAD

Don't assume that everything—or anything—you learn in Torts applies to Criminal Law, and vice versa. Sometimes, that may be the case. The principles may be exactly the same. But usually they are not, as you will see in this case involving the issue of causation.

In this case, a drag race ended in the death of one of the racers who, in an attempt to pass his opponent, crossed the median and was killed when his car was hit by an oncoming truck. The surviving drag racer was accused and convicted of involuntary manslaughter, one element of which was that the accused *caused* the death of his victim.

As you will see, the appellate court refused to apply in the criminal case the broad definition of "proximate cause" that has been used in establishing civil tort liability. Instead, the court ruled, a more direct causal connection is required for conviction of a criminal offense.

COMMONWEALTH OF PENNSYLVANIA v. LEROY W. ROOT
403 Pa. 571, 170 A.2d 310 (1961).

The Court: Leroy Root was found guilty of involuntary manslaughter for the death of his competitor, Lewis Hall, in the course of an automobile race between them on a highway. The testimony discloses that on the night of the fatal accident, the defendant Leroy Root accepted Hall's challenge to engage in an automobile race; that the racing took place on a rural three-lane highway; that the night was clear and dry and traffic was light; that the speed limit on the highway was 50 miles per hour; that, immediately prior to the accident, the two automobiles were being operated at varying speeds of 70 to 90 miles per hour; that the accident occurred in a no-passing zone on the approach to a bridge where the highway narrowed to two directionally opposite lanes; that, at the time of the accident, the defendant Root was in the lead and was proceeding in his right hand lane of travel; that the deceased Hall, in an attempt to pass Root's automobile when a truck was closely approaching from the opposite direction, swerved his car to the left, crossed the highway's white dividing line, and drove his automobile on the wrong side of the highway head-on into the oncoming truck with the resultant fatal effect to himself.

While precedent is to be found for application of the tort law concept of "proximate cause" in fixing responsibility for criminal homicide, the want of any rational basis for its use in determining criminal liability can no longer be properly disregarded. When proximate cause was first borrowed from the field of tort law and applied to homicide prosecutions in Pennsylvania, the concept connoted a much more direct causal relation in producing the alleged culpable result than it does today. Proximate cause, as an essential element of a tort founded in negligence, has undergone in recent times, and is still undergoing, a marked extension. More specifically, this area of civil law has been progressively liberalized in favor of claims for damages for personal injuries to which careless conduct of others can in some way be associated. To persist in applying the tort liability concept of proximate cause to prosecutions for criminal homicide after the marked expansion of civil liability of defendants in tort actions for negligence would be to extend possible criminal liability to persons chargeable with unlawful or reckless conduct in circumstances not generally considered to present the likelihood of a resultant death.

Legal theory that attributes the guilt or innocence of criminal homicide to such accidental and fortuitous circumstances that are now embraced by modern Torts law's encompassing concept of proximate cause is too harsh to be just.

The Torts liability concept of proximate cause has no proper place in prosecutions for criminal homicide, and more direct causal connection is required for conviction. In this case, Root's reckless conduct was not a sufficiently direct cause of the competing driver's death to make him criminally liable.

ANALYSIS

Root was not guilty of involuntary manslaughter because the element of causation was not satisfied as a matter of law. Criminal Law causation is usually more difficult to prove than the Torts notion of "proximate cause." The appellate court reversed the trial court conviction because the prosecution did not establish that Root was the "direct cause" of his competitor's death.

[*NOTE: As you probably noticed, the Root decision as described here has been heavily edited to focus on a single point, and obvious indications of where the edits actually took place are not given. All of the cases excerpted in* Jumpstart Criminal Law *are like that. You should simply realize that there's more to these decisions than what you will find in the excerpts contained in this book.*]

CASE 2. Damages for animal cruelty and neglect: Criminal Law principles are not usually the same as Torts principles, even where some of the terminology is the same; e.g., "negligence." Once again, you must be careful to not try to apply everything—or anything—you learn in Torts to Criminal Law decisions and vice versa.

In this case, Christopher Brunette was convicted of animal cruelty and neglect for abusing his dogs. Brunette asked the court to apportion part of his restitution penalty to the animal shelter agency, which, he argued, had also been negligent. The court refused, concluding that the tort concept of "comparative negligence" simply does not apply to a charge of *criminal* as opposed to civil negligence. Hence, the restitution amount that Brunette was ordered to pay could not be reduced on the grounds that he was arguably not the entire cause of the costs of care of his dogs that the animal welfare agency was forced to incur.

PEOPLE OF CALIFORNIA v. ROBERT CHRISTOPHER BRUNETTE
194 Cal. App.4th 268, 124 Cal. Rptr.3d 521 (Cal. Ct. App. 6 Dist. 2011).

The Court: A jury convicted Brunette of animal cruelty and neglect. The trial court ordered him to pay a large restitution amount to the animal welfare agency that had to arrange care for the dogs it rescued. This appeal requires us to consider whether the trial court erred in not reducing the award to account for the agency's putative comparative negligence in not abating the condition sooner.

Criminal negligence is a more culpable mental state than the negligence that generates tort liability. It is, as a rule, in tort cases that comparative fault principles are applied and there is no reason to depart from that rule here. Ordinary civil negligence standards tend not to apply in the criminal context, although we will stop short of saying that they never do. "Conduct which creates an unreasonable risk of injury to other persons or to their property is generally termed 'ordinary negligence,' a type of fault which will generally serve as the basis for tort liability and occasionally for criminal liability. Conduct which creates not only an unreasonable risk but also a 'high degree' of risk (something more than mere 'unreasonable' risk) may be termed 'gross negligence,' and if in addition the one who creates such a risk realizes that he does so, his conduct may be called 'recklessness.'" Our Supreme Court noted the difference many years ago in discussing involuntary manslaughter: "something more than ordinary negligence is needed to constitute either culpable negligence or criminal negligence under involuntary manslaughter statutes."

In light of these principles, we see no reason to reduce defendant's financial liability, given the relationship between him and his dogs. Defendant wholly controlled the horrific conditions at his forest stronghold and the dogs had no control, except the minimal amount available to establish one or more hierarchies among themselves in fights over food.

The trial court did not err in declining to apportion liability under comparative fault principles. Accordingly, we reject defendant's claim.

ANALYSIS

Brunette was not entitled to a reduced restitution amount due to principles of comparative negligence as comparative negligence is a Torts law concept and does not apply to criminal cases.

CHAPTER 2

Criminal Law: Glossary of Common Legal Terms

Acquittal: An acquittal is a Not Guilty verdict by a jury or a trial judge in a bench trial.

Actus Reus: The actus reus of a crime is the specific criminal act (or acts) that is (or are) criminalized in a criminal offense. *See* Chapter 10. The prosecution must establish the actus reus by proving beyond a reasonable doubt that the accused actually committed the criminal act voluntarily or failed to perform an act that he or she was legally required to perform.

Adversary Proceeding: An adversary proceeding is a contested judicial proceeding in which the prosecution and the defense each have an opportunity to address arguments made by the opposing side. This is in contrast to an "ex parte proceeding" in which only one side makes an argument to a judge and the other side is not present. A criminal trial is a classic example of an adversary proceeding.

Affirmative Defenses: Affirmative defenses provide a defense to charged crimes without the defendant having to negate (in Criminal Law, we often say "negative") an element of the crime. *See* "Elements of the Crime (or Defense)." The defendant, not the prosecution, usually has the burden of introducing evidence proving (usually by a preponderance of the evidence) each of the elements of an affirmative defense. If the defense is successful, the defendant is acquitted or, depending on the statute, his or her offense is sometimes instead "mitigated" to a lower offense, despite the fact that all of the elements of the charged offense may have been established. *See* "Acquittal" and the related discussion in Chapter 7.

American Law Institute's (ALI's) Model Penal Code: *See* "Model Penal Code."

Appeal: The defense may challenge a Guilty verdict on any criminal charge in a higher court by appealing that verdict. The prosecution may not challenge the acquittal of a defendant on factual grounds as such an appeal would violate the constitutional protection against placing a person in double jeopardy, i.e., trying him or her for the same crime twice. *See* "Acquittal."

Appellate Court: An appellate court is a court that considers appeals. *See* "Appeal." Most states have two levels of appellate courts in criminal cases, a mid-level or intermediate appellate court (usually called the Court of Appeals) and a high court (usually called the Supreme Court).

Appellant: The appellant is the party who has appealed. In criminal cases, this is usually the defendant, as the prosecution may not appeal the acquittal of a defendant on factual grounds as such an appeal would violate the constitutional protection against placing a person in double jeopardy, i.e., trying him or her for the same crime twice. Sometimes the appellant is called the petitioner.

Appellate Issue: An appellate issue is a legal question brought to an appellate court's attention by the appellant.

Appellee: The appellee is the party responding to an appeal. In criminal cases, this is usually the prosecution, as the prosecution may not appeal the acquittal of a defendant on factual grounds as such an appeal would violate the constitutional protection against placing a person in double jeopardy, i.e., trying him or her for the same crime twice. Sometimes the appellee is called the respondent.

Arraignment: An arraignment is a court proceeding where an accused person, a defendant, enters a plea (usually guilty or not guilty) to criminal charges. Usually the defendant enters this plea through his or her retained or appointed counsel. *See* Chapter 4.

Arrest: An arrest occurs when a person is involuntarily deprived of his or her liberty by a law enforcement officer. To arrest someone for a crime, an officer needs (1) probable cause that a crime was committed and (2) probable cause that the person to be arrested committed that crime. Unless the offense was a minor crime committed outside of the officer's presence, no arrest warrant is needed. *See* "Probable Cause" and Chapter 4.

Arrest Warrant: An arrest warrant is a document issued by a judge authorizing law enforcement officers to arrest a particular person for a particular crime. *See* "Arrest."

Bail: Bail is a bond that must be posted by a criminal defendant to ensure his or her appearance for court proceedings. A judge determines the amount of bail to be posted. Defendants often use the services of bail bondsmen to post bail. If the defendant does not appear in court when he or she has been ordered to do so, the bail amount is forfeited to the government.

Bench Trial: A trial jury ordinarily decides factual questions of guilt or innocence in a criminal trial. *See* "Jury." But where the defendant waives his or her right to a jury, factual questions are then resolved by the trial judge; this is called a "bench trial." *See* Chapter 5.

Bind Over: If the judge at a preliminary hearing finds that probable cause exists, the defendant is "bound over" on that charge. If not, that charge is dismissed. *See* Chapter 4.

Booking: Arrestees are taken to a police station where they are "booked." Booking is largely a clerical stage in the proceedings where information about the arrestee is gathered and a photograph and fingerprints are taken. The charges on which an arrestee is booked can be—and often are—changed at a later time. *See* Chapter 4.

Burglary: The crime of burglary is typically committed when a person breaks and enters into a building with the intention of committing a felony inside.

Case-in-Chief: The case-in-chief is the portion of a criminal trial where the prosecution presents its evidence against a defendant prior to the defendant's turn to put on his or her evidence and the prosecution's subsequent opportunity to offer rebuttal evidence.

Causation (or Criminal Causation): Causation is often a required element of a criminal offense. *See* "Elements of the Crime (or Defense)." To establish the causation element, the prosecution must establish beyond a reasonable doubt that the accused person's conduct actually caused the criminal result at issue and that that conduct was a legally sufficient cause of the criminal result.

Common Law Crimes: Common Law crimes are a limited set of specifically defined criminal offenses that were available to be prosecuted in the common law courts of England that became a part of the Crimes Code of every U.S. jurisdiction at the time of the founding of this Nation. They include the following offenses: murder, manslaughter, mayhem, rape, larceny, robbery, burglary, arson, assault and battery, perjury, forgery, and bribery. *See* Chapter 8.

Contempt: A trial judge has the power to sanction a lawyer or a person appearing before the court who has engaged in obstructive or contemptuous behavior, e.g., by creating a disruption in the courtroom, by holding him or her "in contempt." Contempt can be punished by fine and/or imprisonment.

Counts: In a criminal prosecution, a count is a distinct criminal charge, e.g., if a defendant has been charged with murdering two people, he or she will go to trial on two counts of murder.

Court: The court is the location of judicial activity, whether trial or appellate. Lawyers also use the term "court" as a synonym for the judge, as in the statement that "the court held . . . ," or "the court ruled. . . ."

Crimes Code: Many of the important criminal statutes, including the most heinous statutory offenses like murder and rape, are often (but not always) collected and codified in each state in the form of a so-called "Crimes Code" or "Penal Code." *See* Chapter 3.

Cross-Examination: The term "cross-examination" refers to the questioning of a witness by the opposing side, e.g., by the prosecution of a defense witness.

Defendant: The person against whom criminal charges have been brought, also referred to often as "the accused."

Discovery: When used in legal proceedings, the discovery process refers to the prescribed process in which the opposing parties (prosecution and defense in the criminal setting) are permitted to discover certain information that the other side possesses prior to trial.

Elements of the Crime (or Defense): Each criminal offense and defense can be broken down into a set of elements, e.g., specified facts that needed to be proved in order to establish the defendant's culpability or innocence. The prosecution must prove every element of a crime beyond a reasonable doubt in order to convict a defendant of that charge. *See* Chapter 6.

Evidence: Evidence consists of those testimonial statements, physical objects, and documents allowed to be presented in a trial court for consideration by the jury or the judge in a bench trial. The rules of evidence govern what testimony or documents may be allowed to be admitted during the trial. For example, witnesses may be allowed to testify as to what they actually saw themselves but may not be allowed to testify about what someone else told them they saw (hearsay).

Ex Parte Proceeding: *See* "Adversary Proceeding."

Exclusionary Rule: Evidence that has been seized unconstitutionally by law enforcement officers is inadmissible in the prosecutor's case-in-chief against a defendant. *See* "Case-in-Chief." This is called the "exclusionary rule," and it is subject to numerous exceptions in application. Nonetheless, its impact is dramatic, as in many criminal cases, incriminating evidence may be suppressed. *See* "Motion to Suppress" and Chapter 4.

Exculpatory: Evidence is deemed to be "exculpatory" in a criminal case when it tends to create a doubt about the accused person's culpability. In contrast, evidence is deemed to be "incriminating" or "inculpatory" in a criminal case when it tends to confirm or establish the accused person's culpability.

Failure-of-Proof Defenses: Failure-of-proof defenses comprise the most common kind of defense in criminal cases. Defense counsel defends his or her client by establishing that the prosecution has not carried its burden of proving one or more elements of the crime beyond a reasonable doubt. *See* Chapter 7.

Felony: A felony is the most serious category of criminal offense, often punishable by a potential sentence of more than 6 months in prison.

First-Degree Murder: First-degree murder, sometimes called "premeditated murder," is an intentional killing undertaken with malice that is premeditated, willful, and deliberate. *See* "Murder."

Flipper: "Flipper" is a slang term for a codefendant who decides to testify against one or more of his or her former codefendants in exchange for being treated more leniently by the prosecution.

General Deterrence: Criminalization based upon the idea of general deterrence reflects the belief that by punishing wrong-doers, society will benefit by keeping others from committing (deterring) the commission of future crimes. So, while specific deterrence focuses on a specific convicted individual, general deterrence is intended to serve broader goals, acting as an example to any other potential criminals about the risks of engaging in this kind of criminal behavior. *See* Chapter 8.

Grand Jury: A grand jury is a jury of 12 to 23 persons convened to evaluate accusations of criminality against persons and to determine whether the evidence warrants prosecution. A relic from the English Common Law, grand juries only exist for this purpose in federal prosecutions and in a handful of states. In these jurisdictions, instead of or in addition to a preliminary examination, the prosecution makes a secret presentation of evidence. If the grand jury finds probable cause to exist, it issues a grand jury indictment. Grand jury proceedings are secret. *See* "Jury," "Preliminary Hearing," "Probable Cause," and Chapter 4.

Guideline Sentencing: *See* "Sentencing Guidelines."

Guilt: Guilt means criminal culpability, e.g., a jury finds the defendant guilty of the charged crimes.

Guilty Plea: *See* "Pleas."

Habeas Corpus: A writ of habeas corpus is a post-conviction judicial order that a convicted person be freed because he or she was subjected to a violation of his or her constitutional rights by the state courts. *See* "Post-Conviction Relief."

Harmless Error: No trial is perfect, criminal or civil. Often an appellate court will find that some sort of error or errors occurred at trial but will, nonetheless, affirm a conviction because the error was judged not to have affected the fundamental fairness of the proceeding.

Holding: A holding is an appellate court's answer to a legal question. An appellate court may affirm, reverse, or modify the decision of a lower court.

Homicide: Homicide is the generic term of art used to describe the particular killing acts that have been criminalized in a particular jurisdiction, e.g., murder and manslaughter.

Hung Jury: When jurors cannot agree on a verdict, the jury is said to be a "hung jury." When a jury has been hung, the prosecution has the right—but not the obligation—to bring the same charges once again in a new trial with a new and different jury. *See* "Jury" and Chapter 5.

Incapacitation: *See* "Specific Deterrence."

Indictment: An indictment is a document issued by a grand jury that charges an accused with the commission of one or more criminal offenses. *See* Chapter 4.

Indigents: The majority of criminal defendants in the United States are too poor to post bail or to afford an attorney. These people are called "indigents." There is no constitutional definition of who is poor enough to count as an indigent. Each jurisdiction decides that for itself. *See* "Bail."

Information: Used in its legal sense, an "information" is a document issued after a preliminary hearing that charges an accused with the commission of one or more criminal offenses. *See* "Preliminary Hearing" and Chapter 4.

Innocence: *See* "Acquittal."

Instructions: After the prosecution and the defense have presented their evidence at a criminal trial and made their closing arguments, the trial judge delivers "instructions" to the jury. The judge determines the applicable law, and then he or she instructs the jury about what law to apply to the case before it. *See* Chapter 5.

Involuntary Manslaughter: Involuntary manslaughter is a common homicide offense, usually defined as an unintentional killing that has been committed without malice. *See* "Malice."

IRAC: The acronym IRAC stands for one of the most effective ways to review, analyze, and prepare appellate court decisions for understanding them and for discussion in class. The letters stand for **I**ssue, **R**ule, **A**nalysis, and **C**onclusion. *See* Chapter 9.

Jurisdiction: The term "jurisdiction" has two different meanings. One is a governmental entity possessing power over the lives and conduct of the individuals living there, e.g., a state or the federal government. The second meaning is the scope of the authority and control possessed, e.g., a state usually has jurisdiction only over criminal conduct that has occurred within the physical confines of that state.

Jury: A criminal trial jury is a group of ordinary citizens selected to evaluate questions of fact and to reach a verdict on the basis of the evidence presented to them about the guilt or innocence of a criminal defendant. *See* Chapter 5. Where the defendant waives his or her right to a jury, factual questions are then resolved by the trial judge. *See* "Bench Trial."

Jury Nullification: Jury nullification is the name given to the attempt by defense counsel to sway the jurors to one degree or another by presenting a narrative to them that might cause them to sympathize with the accused and "nullify" the law and the jury instructions by ignoring them. *See* Chapters 5 and 7.

Knowing Conduct: Knowing conduct is often treated as a specific type of mens rea element. *See* "Mens Rea." Often, in Criminal Law, this refers to an individual's awareness that his or her conduct is practically certain to cause a criminal result, e.g., the death of another person.

Malice: Malice is a term of art from the English Common Law that refers to a particularly heinous ill will on the part of a killer. It is the distinguishing factor between murder and manslaughter offenses in most jurisdictions.

Mandatory Minimums: Mandatory minimums are a statutory sentencing requirement where a defendant convicted of a particular crime or of a particular act in committing a specified crime (e.g., carrying a firearm) must receive a minimum sentence of incarceration. Although the sentencing judge has discretion in determining the upper range of the sentence, he or she has no discretion to diverge from the required minimum sentence. *See* Chapter 4.

Mens Rea: The mens rea of a crime is the specific criminal intention (sometimes called "scienter" by courts) that is required to be proved to establish commission of a particular criminal offense. "Mens rea" is the Latin term for "guilty mind." *See* Chapter 10. Sometimes, legislatures do not require proof of a criminal intention. That type of criminal statute is called strict liability. *See* "Strict Liability Offenses."

Misdemeanor: A misdemeanor is a less serious category of criminal offense (in contrast to the more serious category of felonies), often punishable by fine and/or a potential sentence of less than 6 months in prison. *See* "Felony."

Model Penal Code: The Model Penal Code (MPC), a model Crimes Code, was adopted by the American Law Institute (ALI) in 1962. The MPC provisions are not precedential law in and of themselves. In fact, some MPC provisions were never adopted by any state, and others are outdated by now, especially the provisions relating to sex crimes. But many states have enacted significant portions of the MPC as a part of their own Crimes Codes, and courts continue to refer to MPC provisions and commentary in interpreting criminal statutes. As a result, the MPC remains an important reference point for understanding Criminal Law in the United States. *See* Chapters 6 and 8.

Motions: The prosecution and defense may bring legal issues to the trial judge for resolution by making a "motion" or "moving" to obtain a particular result or ruling. Motions may be written or oral depending on the circumstances. The judge either denies or grants a motion. The most important motion in criminal proceedings is a "motion to suppress." *See* "Motion to Suppress."

Motion to Suppress: Evidence that has been seized unconstitutionally by law enforcement officers is inadmissible in the prosecutor's case-in-chief against a defendant. This is called the "exclusionary rule," and it is subject to numerous exceptions in application. Defense counsel raises this issue with a motion to suppress the relevant evidence, and this motion is heard in a pretrial hearing, called a suppression hearing. *See* "Motions," "Exclusionary Rule," "Suppression Hearing," and Chapter 4.

Murder: Murder is a killing of another human being committed with malice. *See* "Malice."

Negligence (or Criminal Negligence or Gross Negligence): Negligence (often referred to as criminal or gross negligence in Criminal Law) is a specific type of mens rea element. *See* "Mens Rea." Often, in Criminal Law, it refers to an individual's actions when he or she should have been aware of a substantial and unjustifiable risk that a specified result (e.g., someone's death) would result from his or her conduct. In addition, that risk must reflect a gross deviation from what a reasonable person would have done in those circumstances.

Nolo Contendere Plea: Essentially a "nolo plea" or pleading "no contest" is an admission of culpability, but the accused is still not expressly admitting his or her actual guilt in the matter. A nolo contendere plea is, however, treated by the court like a Guilty plea. *See* "Pleas" and Chapter 4.

Not Guilty Plea: *See* "Pleas."

Opinion: A judicial opinion is a judge's formal explanation, usually in writing, stating the basis for a judicial decision.

Order: When a judge directs that something must be done or not done, that directive is called an "order." An order can be as limited as directing a witness to answer certain questions on penalty of contempt or it can affect the entire prosecution as, for example, an order dismissing one or more criminal charges.

Penal Code: *See* "Crimes Code."

Petitioner: *See* "Appellant."

Pleas: An accused person, called the defendant, must enter a response to criminal charges filed against him or her, and this response is called a "plea." The three possible pleas that may be entered are Guilty, Not Guilty, and Nolo Contendere. A defendant might also simply "stand mute," i.e., he or she refuses to enter any plea at all, in which case a Not Guilty pleas is entered for him or her. Usually the defendant enters his or her plea through defense counsel. *See* Chapter 4.

Plea Bargaining: Plea bargaining is a process whereby criminal defense counsel and a prosecutor reach a mutually agreeable disposition of criminal charges subject to court approval. *See* Chapter 4.

Post-Conviction Relief: Once a convicted defendant's appeals have been concluded, his or her conviction is "final." But he or she may still challenge the conviction at a later point in post-conviction proceedings. One of the most common forms of post-conviction proceeding is a petition for a writ of habeas corpus, which can be filed in federal court by a defendant who was convicted in a state court and has exhausted his or her direct appeals. A writ of habeas corpus is a judicial order that a convicted person be freed because he or she was subjected to a violation of his or her constitutional rights by the state courts. *See* Chapter 4 and "Habeas Corpus."

Preliminary Hearing: A preliminary hearing (sometimes called a preliminary examination) is a pretrial adversary proceeding at which the prosecution must establish that there is probable cause to support each and every charge it has brought against the defendant. If the judge finds probable cause to exist, the defendant is "bound over" on that charge. If not, that charge is dismissed. *See* "Probable Cause," "Adversary Proceeding," and Chapter 4.

Premeditated Murder: *See* "First-Degree Murder."

Presentment: The U.S. Constitution requires that an arrested individual be brought before a magistrate "promptly." This initial appearance is called different things in different jurisdictions, most commonly, the "presentment." (In some states, it is called the "preliminary arraignment" or the "arraignment on the warrant.") *See* Chapter 4.

Pretrial Intervention Program: Pretrial intervention programs (often short-handed to "PTI") provide persons accused of particular minor crimes, usually first offenders, an opportunity to avoid trial on those charges by participating in rehabilitative programs for a set period of time without getting into further trouble with the law. If the participants accomplish this successfully, the charges are dropped. If they cannot, the charges are reinstated, and prosecution results.

Prima Facie Case: In criminal cases, a "prima facie case" is a showing by the prosecution sufficient to avoid dismissal of the charges prior to trial on the merits.

Probable Cause: Probable cause is a fair probability that a crime was committed and the individual to be arrested committed that crime. To arrest someone for a crime, an officer needs (1) probable cause that a crime was committed and (2) probable cause that the person to be arrested committed that crime. *See* "Arrest."

Prosecution: The prosecution is the government agency that brings and tries criminal charges against accused persons. State prosecutors, often called District Attorneys, are usually elected officials.

Purposeful (or Intentional) Conduct: Purposeful or intentional conduct is often treated as a specific type of mens rea element. *See* "Mens Rea." Often, in Criminal Law, it refers to an individual's conscious object to cause a criminal result, e.g., the death of another person.

Quashed: When a court is said to "quash" something (e.g., an appeal or an indictment), it is dismissing it or "throwing it out."

Recklessness: Recklessness is a specific type of mens rea element. *See* "Mens Rea." Often, in Criminal Law, it refers to an individual's conscious disregard of a substantial and unjustifiable risk that a specified result (e.g., someone's death) will result from his or her conduct, and that disregard must be a gross deviation from what a reasonable person would have done in those circumstances.

Rehabilitation: Criminalization of conduct based upon the idea of rehabilitation reflects the belief that convicted criminals can be "cured" during incarceration and then returned to society, no longer posing a threat to others. The hope is that through appropriate treatment, criminal offenders will be encouraged or trained to reenter society as productive citizens. *See* Chapter 8.

Remand: A remand is an order by an appellate court sending the case back to a lower court. A remand may include additional instructions to the lower court judge detailing what steps that judge must take with the case. The term "remand" is also used on occasion to refer to the act of returning a defendant to custody pending trial or simply for further detention.

Restraint: *See* "Specific Deterrence."

Respondent: *See* "Appellee."

Retribution: Criminalization based upon the idea of retribution reflects the belief that society must punish criminals because that is precisely what they deserve ("just deserts") or in order to exact vengeance for the wrong-doer's criminal acts. In the Old Testament of the Bible, this was called "an eye for an eye." *See* Chapter 8.

Robbery: Robbery is a crime involving the use or threat of violence or force while an actor is committing a theft of property.

Scienter: *See* "Mens Rea."

Search Warrant: A search warrant is a document issued by a judge authorizing law enforcement officers to search specific premises for specific items connected with criminal activity.

Second-Degree Murder: Second-degree murder is typically defined as a killing act undertaken with malice but without the premeditation and deliberation necessary to establish first-degree murder. *See* "Malice" and "First-Degree Murder."

Sentencing Guidelines: Guideline sentencing is a system in which every criminal offense is assigned a numerical point score and points are then added or subtracted to that score on the basis of a sentencing judge's finding that specified aggravating or mitigating factors are present. Depending on the final point total, the judge sentences from a range that has been assigned to that specific point total. *See* Chapter 4.

Snitch: *See* "Flipper."

Specific Deterrence: Criminalization based upon the idea of specific deterrence (also called "restraint" or "incapacitation") reflects the belief that criminal punishment is desirable in order to confine or isolate convicted criminals to prevent them from committing additional criminal acts. Additionally, the idea is that by punishing this particular ("specific") criminal, he or she will realize the seriousness of his or her antisocial behavior and will be deterred from committing future crimes as a result. *See* Chapter 8.

Statutes: A statute is a law that has been enacted by a legislative body.

Strict Liability Offenses: The mens rea of a crime is the specific criminal intention that is required to be proved to establish commission of a particular criminal offense. Sometimes, legislatures do not require proof of a criminal intention. If the prosecution need not prove any specific criminal intention, that type of criminal statute is called a strict liability offense. *See* Chapter 10.

Suppression Hearing: A suppression hearing is just what it sounds like, namely a hearing where the defense is attempting to suppress evidence that may be used at trial against the defendant. Evidence that has been seized unconstitutionally by law enforcement is inadmissible in the prosecutor's case-in-chief against a defendant. This is the "exclusionary rule," although it is subject to many exceptions in application. Defense counsel raises this issue with a motion to suppress particular evidence, and this motion is heard in a pretrial hearing, called a suppression hearing. *See* "Motions," "Exclusionary Rule," "Motion to Suppress," and Chapter 4.

Trial Court: The trial court is the court where the criminal trial is held and where fact questions are decided (usually) by a jury.

Verdict: The verdict is the decision by the jury (or by the trial judge in a bench trial) on the question of the accused person's guilt or innocence.

CHAPTER 3

Context: Jurisdictional Variance and Dual Sovereignty

A. JURISDICTIONAL VARIANCE

Every U.S. jurisdiction—every state, the District of Columbia, each U.S. territory, and the federal government itself—has its own unique and idiosyncratic set of criminal statutes.

Many of the important criminal statutes, including the most heinous statutory offenses like murder and rape, are often (but not always) collected and codified in each state in the form of a so-called "Crimes Code" or "Penal Code."

Although every state's Crimes Code is different, there are nonetheless lots of similarities between criminal statutes that cover the very same subject state by state. Indeed, some criminal offenses are virtually identical in different states. For example, first-degree murder statutes often punish the same or very similar homicidal conduct—premeditated killings.

Take a look, for example, at Michigan's, Pennsylvania's, and Nevada's first-degree murder statutes:

- Mich. C. L. §750.316(1)(a) ("A person who commits any of the following is guilty of first degree murder[:] Murder perpetrated by means of poison, lying in wait, or any other willful, deliberate, and premeditated killing.")
- Pa. C. S. §2502(a) ("A criminal homicide constitutes murder of the first degree when it is committed by [k]illing by means of poison, or by lying in wait, or by any other kind of willful, deliberate and premeditated killing.")
- Nev. R. S. §200.030(1)(a) ("Murder of the first degree is murder which is . . . [p]erpetrated by means of poison, lying in wait or torture, or by any other kind of willful, deliberate and premeditated killing.")

These statutes are almost identical, aren't they?

But you should recognize that such similarities exist only because the legislatures in those states want their laws to be that way. Short of a constitutional prohibition of some sort, legislatures have the sovereign power to criminalize or not to criminalize virtually anything they want and to create whatever exceptions they desire for those criminalized activities.

For example, let's say that the Texas legislature decides to criminalize the use of interactive wireless communications devices, such as BlackBerries, iPhones, and other smartphones, while a person is driving. Of course, the Texas legislature has the sovereign power to do just that—to criminalize that activity.

And if South Dakota decides to criminalize the very same activities, but the legislators in that state decide to create an exception, say, for "a device being used exclusively as a global positioning or navigation system or a system or device that is physically or electronically integrated into the vehicle," well, South Dakota is perfectly free to do just that.

Subsequently, if Mississippi legislators, in contrast, discuss the very same issue, but they choose not to criminalize texting while driving at all, then that is a choice that Mississippi is perfectly entitled to make. Again, each state is sovereign in this respect.

B. THE CRIMINAL LAW KEEPS CHANGING

Not only are all states' criminal statutes potentially different from one another, but they all keep changing, too. Legislatures keep enacting new criminal statutes. And they are continually repealing or amending existing criminal statutes as well.

For example, using the example just described, if the legislature in South Dakota subsequently decides to create another exception to its texting-while-driving statute to exclude, say, "a communications device that is affixed to a mass transit vehicle, bus, or school bus," then it can certainly do just that. This might happen, by the way, at the very same time that Texas decides to repeal its statute entirely and that Washington State decides to newly enact the very same statutory language Texas just repealed.

The point is that criminal statutes in every jurisdiction are a "moving target," i.e., new ones are constantly being enacted, and existing ones are constantly being repealed or amended.

Notably, sometimes, a statutory change is made in direct response to court decisions. A state court might, for example, interpret a criminal statute in a particular way, and the legislature might "respond" by amending the statute. For example, a court might hold that the existing crime of "assault on a police officer" does not apply by its terms to part-time police officers.

Some legislators might then decide that the statute should apply to part-timers. As a result, they might introduce a bill to that effect, and the legislature might eventually "respond" (this usually does not happen quickly) by amending the statute to make it expressly apply to part-time police officers, too. And then—who knows?—the issue may arise of whether the statute applies to off-duty officers, and the courts will weigh in, and the legislature may respond to that . . . and the process goes on and on.

C. WHY ARE STATE CRIMINAL STATUTES OFTEN SIMILAR?

The similarities between criminal statutes covering the same activity in different states are not something that has happened by chance or coincidence. There are a number of good reasons for why criminal statutes covering the same conduct are identical or very similar in different jurisdictions. These reasons include the following:

- In all of the American states, except Louisiana, the earliest criminal offenses were based to some degree on identical Common Law crimes. *See* the discussion in Chapter 8. (This reason explains the similarity between the Michigan, Pennsylvania, and Nevada first-degree murder statutes set out above.) Louisiana law, in contrast, is unique in that it has French origins dating back to the Napoleonic Code.
- Many state (and some federal) criminal offenses and defenses were derived in whole or in part from the very same source: ALI's MPC, which was promulgated in 1962. As a result, to the extent that a state has "borrowed" the MPC approach in a particular area, its statute may look just like the other states that decided to take the same approach and enact the very same MPC language.
- State legislatures often "copy" from one another. If, for example, Ohio enacts a new criminal statute that criminalizes the failure by Little League coaches to report cases of suspected child abuse, legislators in neighboring states, like Illinois and Indiana, might think that that is a really good idea. As a result, these states might introduce similar legislation, resulting in the enactment of similar (or identical) legislation in all three states. There's nothing wrong with this kind of "copying," of course. Why not borrow good ideas from another state?
- Special interest groups, like the National Rifle Association, right-to-life groups, gun-control lobbies, and labor unions, for example, each with special expertise in areas of the law of particular interest to them, will often draft "model" legislation in their areas of interest. Subsequently,

legislators sympathetic to those particular interests may introduce these model laws as actual bills in their state legislatures. As a result, some of these legislative proposals, drafted initially by private interest groups, will end up being enacted into law in one or a number of different states. Of course, it often happens that new statutes like these have been amended sufficiently and differently in each state during the legislative process such that the enacted versions of the same original proposed legislation may differ significantly from one another.

D. DUAL SOVEREIGNTY: THE FEDERAL GOVERNMENT AND THE STATES CAN CRIMINALIZE AND PROSECUTE THE SAME CONDUCT

As discussed previously, every U.S. jurisdiction has the power to enact its own unique set of criminal offenses and defenses. That includes each and every state in the United States. But in our system of federalism, the federal government is also a separate sovereign jurisdiction in its own right.

Congress possesses the power to and has prohibited criminal activities that relate to federal interests, e.g., crimes involving national security, crimes committed on federal property like military bases or post offices, criminal acts targeting federal employees, and crimes involving multistate activity that would be difficult for a single state to police effectively, such as interstate organized crime activities.

Significantly, because the federal government is distinct from each state government and because each is sovereign in its own sphere, criminal conduct that takes place within a state can be punished *both* by state criminal authorities and by federal authorities without running afoul of any constitutional double jeopardy protections. This is the concept of "dual sovereignty."

For example, if X robs a post office, that's a federal criminal offense. *See* 18 U.S.C. §2115 ("Whoever forcibly breaks into or attempts to break into any post office, or any building used in whole or in part as a post office, with intent to commit in such post office, or building or part thereof, so used, any larceny or other depredation, shall be fined under this title or imprisoned not more than five years, or both."). Obviously, since the Postal Service is a federal agency, that activity implicates federal interests.

But that very same conduct—robbing a post office—is also a state offense in the state where the robbery occurred. It's a robbery, just like any other robbery, even though it was aimed at a federal agency. As a result, X can—theoretically, at least—be tried and convicted twice, by *both* federal and state prosecutors simultaneously or in one prosecution after the other.

Usually, however, although two prosecutions are theoretically possible, that just won't happen. Usually, only one of the two sovereigns—the federal authorities or the state authorities—will prosecute someone in X's situation, and that will be it. But the point is that *both* the federal government and the state government have the right and the power to bring their own prosecutions in such a case. And sometimes this occurs, often in cases involving alleged deprivations of civil rights where a state law enforcement officer has been previously acquitted in a state court but the federal Department of Justice believes that the officer engaged in criminal conduct despite his or her state court acquittal.

E. MOST CRIMES ARE PROSECUTED IN STATE COURTS

The U.S. Attorneys in the 94 U.S. Attorney's Offices around the country usually prosecute only those offenses that they believe have a clear tie to federal interests or that are appropriate targets for prosecution under prevailing Department of Justice guidelines and policy.

As a result, despite the existence of overlapping federal and state criminal authority and jurisdiction, more than 95 percent of the crimes committed in the United States—crimes like murders, sexual assaults, robberies, assaults, narcotics offenses, and thefts—are prosecuted at the state level or in the District of Columbia, not by federal prosecutors in federal courts.

CHAPTER 4

Context: Steps in the Criminal Justice Process

Reading and understanding Criminal Law decisions is much easier when you have some familiarity with the chronology and substance of the proceedings that take place during the criminal justice process. What's a preliminary hearing, for example, and what does the prosecution have to prove there? When is an accused defendant indicted, if ever? What's an arraignment?

These procedural steps in the criminal justice process are the backdrop for the court's resolution of substantive Criminal Law questions. It makes all the difference in the world, for example, if an appellate court is assessing the legitimacy of a conviction on appeal or instead is ruling on the question whether a trial judge properly quashed a criminal indictment or information for failure to make out a prima facie case of criminal conduct. Why does it make a difference? To answer that question, you need some background.

What follows is an extremely concise and bare-bones, step-by-step description of the criminal process in a typical U.S. jurisdiction where a serious crime is at issue.

A. FIRST STEP: REPORT OR INVESTIGATION

Criminal arrests and prosecutions result either from a report about a crime having been committed (e.g., a 911 call is made by an eyewitness reporting a burglary in progress) or they are the product of information that was discovered in a police or prosecutorial investigation.

The overwhelming majority of criminal activity, however, comes to the attention of the police the first way—through a report by an individual or an observation made by a police officer. This means that most arrests of individuals for criminal activity are reactive, not proactive. The police are responding to a reported crime or something they have seen or have been told is happening; neither they nor prosecutors initiated an investigation that produced information leading to arrests.

B. SECOND STEP: ARREST

[handwritten margin note: if no warrant if 2 elements met]

To arrest someone for a crime, a police officer needs (1) probable cause that a crime was committed and (2) probable cause that the person to be arrested committed that crime. Unless the offense was a minor crime committed outside of the officer's presence, no arrest warrant is needed.

But, significantly, law enforcement officers in this country have the discretion of whether or not to arrest a person who they believe has committed a crime. They don't have to make that arrest. Many minor crimes, such as jaywalking, petty theft, or littering, are ignored by police officers, and lawfully so. However, the fact that officers have such discretion sometimes leads to claims that such discretion is exercised in a discriminatory fashion.

C. THIRD STEP: BOOKING

Arrestees are taken to a police station where they are "booked." Booking is largely a clerical stage in the proceedings where information about the arrestee is gathered from him or her and from elsewhere (e.g., from computerized law enforcement networks) and a photograph and fingerprints are taken. The charges on which an arrestee is booked can be changed at a later time. Indeed, that is a common occurrence, namely that charges are later dropped or new charges are added.

People arrested for minor crimes will sometimes be released relatively quickly, although they may have to post bail as security that they will return to face the charges. If, however, the arrested person is going to be kept in jail for any period of time, he or she is usually subjected to a full-body search, and his or her possessions are taken from him or her and inventoried.

D. FOURTH STEP: DECISION TO PROSECUTE

After someone has been arrested, a prosecutor still needs to make the decision of whether or not to actually prosecute that person. The decision to prosecute is not a police officer's decision; it's a prosecutor's decision. And, like the police officer's discretion of whether or not to arrest, a prosecutor has complete discretion of whether or not to prosecute.

There are many, many reasons why the discretionary decision might be made to not prosecute an arrested person for a crime, including, but by no means limited to, the following:

- Although there may (or may not) have been probable cause to make an arrest, a prosecutor may believe that there is just not enough evidence to establish the arrestee's guilt beyond a reasonable doubt at trial.

- There are not enough witnesses available to testify, or the witnesses who are available lack credibility or have other problems that diminish their value to the prosecution.
- The arresting officers may have engaged in misconduct in making the arrest or searching officers may have engaged in misconduct when searching for and discovering evidence.
- The offense is deemed to be relatively minor, and the arrestee is viewed as having "suffered enough."
- The arrestee has agreed to plead guilty to another charge or charges in exchange for this charge being dropped.
- The arrestee has agreed to participate in a pretrial intervention program in order to escape prosecution.

As many as 40 percent of all arrestees are released at this point, without ever being prosecuted for the crime for which they were arrested. If the decision is made, however, to go ahead with a prosecution, a criminal complaint is filed that lists the charges being brought against the defendant.

E. FIFTH STEP: INITIAL APPEARANCE

The U.S. Constitution requires that an arrested individual be brought before a magistrate "promptly," although this could take as much as a couple of days. This initial appearance is called different things in different jurisdictions, such as the "presentment," the "preliminary arraignment," or the "arraignment on the warrant."

The reason for the existence of this step is to create an opportunity for a preliminary check on whether the arrested person has been lawfully detained. No one should be held in jail without proper justification. Until this point in the proceeding—in an ordinary case—no judicial officer has taken a look at this matter. Only police officers and prosecutors have been involved.

Bail may be required at this point, but the majority of criminal defendants are poor ("indigents"). If bail is set and the defendant cannot afford (or is otherwise unable) to post it, he or she will be held in jail until further proceedings take place. More than half of the people in jails in the United States have not been convicted of the crime for which they are incarcerated. They have not been able to post bail and are therefore stuck there, waiting for their trials to begin.

At the initial appearance, the accused defendant is also informed of the charges filed against him or her and told what rights he or she has, including—if he or she is indigent—the right to counsel. This stage of the criminal process is usually not an adversary proceeding, i.e., it is not contested by the defense. Unless the accused has retained private counsel, no attorney participates on his or her behalf. Again, most defendants are indigent and cannot afford to hire their own private defense counsel.

F. SIXTH (AND VERY IMPORTANT) STEP: PRELIMINARY HEARING

This is a very important step in the criminal process. This is an adversary proceeding at which the prosecution must establish that there is probable cause (both that a crime has been committed and that the accused committed it) to support each and every charge it has brought against the defendant. If the judge finds such probable cause to exist, the defendant is "bound over" on that charge. If not, that charge is dismissed.

Obviously, the preliminary hearing (or sometimes, it is called a "preliminary examination") is extremely important as a stage at which the proceedings can continue or be terminated. But it is even more important than that. The preliminary hearing is the criminal defendant's primary "discovery" tool.

In civil cases, the discovery stage has become the centerpiece of civil litigation. Prior to a civil trial—if one ever takes place—the opposing sides engage in a vigorous and often extensive discovery process, including filing interrogatories and requests for admissions, taking depositions, and otherwise attempting to find out "all of the cards" the other side is holding. But these discovery tools are usually unavailable in criminal proceedings.

Other than the prosecution's constitutional obligation to turn over to the defense certain, limited exculpatory information (information that may assist in exonerating the accused), there is virtually no discovery at all in criminal proceedings. No discovery . . . *except* for the information garnered by the defense during the preliminary examination. Because of the importance of this discovery role, indigent defendants have the right to have appointed counsel present and participating at this stage.

The prosecution must put on enough of a case at this stage, including witnesses, to convince a judge that probable cause exists to continue the prosecution. The defense, as a result, has the opportunity to hear and assess a good part (although not all) of the prosecution's case, including the right to view the documents introduced into evidence and to cross examine the prosecution witnesses presented. That, in short, is the defense's discovery. (The defense rarely puts on any case at this stage other than cross examining the prosecution's witnesses.)

If the defendant is bound over on charges presented at the preliminary examination, the prosecution files a charging document called a criminal "information," which supplants the criminal complaint.

G. SEVENTH (ALTERNATE/MINORITY JURISDICTION) STEP: GRAND JURY

[handwritten: 8 states, sometimes Missouri & NY ALL fed crimes]

In federal cases, and in (only) a handful of state jurisdictions, an institution called the grand jury exists to serve a similar charging function as the preliminary examination. In these jurisdictions, either instead of a preliminary examination or in addition to a preliminary examination (depending on the jurisdiction), the prosecution makes an ex parte (i.e., one side only appearing) presentation of evidence, including witness testimony, to the grand jurors, who are selected in the same fashion as ordinary trial jurors. If and when these grand jurors find probable cause to exist with respect to criminal charges, instead of an information issuing, a grand jury indictment results.

Unlike a preliminary hearing, grand jury proceedings are *secret*. Witnesses before the grand jury are not allowed to have lawyers with them in the grand jury room. Prosecutors make ex parte (uncontested) presentations of evidence and examinations of witnesses, unlike the adversary manner of proceeding in a preliminary examination. Witnesses must testify unless they claim that their answers to questions posed will tend to incriminate them. But even in that case, where a witness declines to testify on the grounds that it may incriminate him, the prosecution may "immunize" the witness—agree not to prosecute him for his testimony, in which case, he must testify or risk being held in contempt and face the possibility of being sent to jail. Although the defendant will receive a transcript of the grand jury proceedings after the fact, defense counsel does not have the same discovery advantages of subjecting the prosecution's witnesses to cross examination in front of the grand jurors.

H. EIGHTH (POSSIBLE) STEP: PLEA NEGOTIATION

Plea bargaining can take place at any stage of the criminal proceedings, but this is a common time when it may occur. Although such "bargaining" may seem unseemly or inappropriate to some people, the entry of a Guilty plea as a result of negotiations and a "plea agreement" made by the prosecutor and defense counsel is in fact the most common resolution of a criminal prosecution that has not otherwise ended in an early dismissal.

Although it didn't always take this position, the Supreme Court during the last four decades has recognized the systemic value and importance of plea bargaining, commenting as follows in 1971:

> The disposition of criminal charges by agreement between the prosecutor and the accused, sometimes loosely called 'plea bargaining,' is an essential component of the administration of justice. Properly administered, it is to be encouraged. If every criminal charge were subjected to a full-scale trial, the States and

plea bargains encouraged

the Federal Government would need to multiply by many times the number of judges and court facilities.

Disposition of charges after plea discussions is not only an essential part of the process but a highly desirable part for many reasons. It leads to prompt and largely final disposition of most criminal cases; it avoids much of the corrosive impact of enforced idleness during pre-trial confinement for those who are denied release pending trial; it protects the public from those accused persons who are prone to continue criminal conduct even while on pretrial release; and, by shortening the time between charge and disposition, it enhances whatever may be the rehabilitative prospects of the guilty when they are ultimately imprisoned.[1]

Practically speaking, from a prosecutor's point of view, a plea agreement creates certainty; it guarantees a conviction. It eliminates the risk—always present—that an accused person will go free. Who knows what a jury might decide to do?

And from the defendant's point of view, a plea bargain creates certainty as well; it reduces the risk of conviction on additional counts or on a more serious count. Or it ensures or optimizes the chance of the defendant receiving a lighter sentence than he or she might otherwise have received. So, in that sense, it reduces risk to the defendant, too; that is, the risk of harsher consequences.

In practice, a defendant entering a Guilty plea to criminal charges as a result of a negotiated plea agreement must make clear on the record just what he or she believes he is receiving in exchange for the plea. This takes place in what is called a "Guilty plea colloquy."

Similarly, the prosecutor must acknowledge on the record what he or she has offered the defendant in exchange for that plea. In this way, there should be no misunderstanding about the nature of "the deal" that has been reached by the parties. And, as a result, if one of the parties fails to follow through on the agreement, the plea deal can be cancelled and the defendant will have to stand trial.

For example, a common plea-bargained agreement requires a defendant to plead guilty to a lesser charge in exchange, among other things (lawyers and judges often say instead "inter alia" instead of "among other things"), for her cooperation in testifying against a former criminal accomplice. If the defendant fails to live up to her part of that bargain—that is, if she perjures herself at her confederate's trial or if she refuses to testify altogether (and both of these things happen)—the original plea deal can and probably will be abrogated by the same court that heard the Guilty plea colloquy.

---

1. Santobello v. New York, 404 U.S. 257, 260-61 (1971).

I. NINTH STEP: ARRAIGNMENT AND PLEAS

Until this point, the accused defendant has not had to enter a plea. Now that there's a charging document to which to respond—an information or an indictment—the defendant (usually through his or her retained or appointed counsel) needs to enter a plea. There are three possible pleas that may be entered:

- Guilty
- Not Guilty
- Nolo Contendere

A defendant might also simply "stand mute," i.e., refuse to enter any plea at all.

Most defendants enter a Guilty plea at this point (or later on in the process). The reason for that result is discussed in the prior step in the process, namely, that Guilty pleas are most often the result of negotiated plea bargains. When a Guilty plea is proffered by the defendant, he or she must then concede in open court that he or she is guilty of every element of each of the charges to which he or she is pleading.

Significantly, the judge receiving a Guilty plea has the discretion of whether or not to accept the plea. If the judge believes that the plea bargain is too generous to the accused, the judge may decline to accept it. In 1991, for example, the federal judge hearing a criminal case against Exxon, arising out of the 1989 Exxon Valdez oil spill off the coast of Alaska, refused to accept a $100 million criminal fine agreed to by Exxon and government lawyers in a plea-bargained arrangement, ruling that the fine was much too low.

[handwritten margin note: if sentence too low, deny guilty plea]

With the permission of the prosecution, an accused might—instead of a Guilty plea—enter a plea of "nolo contendere," Latin for "I do not contest." Essentially a "nolo plea," or pleading "no contest," is an admission of culpability, but the accused is still not expressly admitting his or her actual guilt in the matter. Nonetheless, a nolo plea is treated by the court in the same fashion as if the accused actually pleads guilty.

In particular, a person entering a nolo plea must participate in exactly the same sort of colloquy as with a Guilty plea, conceding to the judge in open court that he or she is not contesting each and every element of each of the charges to which he or she is pleading.

Moreover, a person pleading nolo contendere will be sentenced in the same way and to the same extent as if he or she had simply pleaded guilty instead. There may also be some value to the defendant of being permitted to enter a nolo plea. In some jurisdictions, a nolo contendere plea may not be used to establish liability in subsequent civil proceedings that arise out of the same facts underlying the criminal proceedings.

If a person pleads not guilty to criminal charges, those charges are then set for trial. And when a person stands mute, refusing to plead at all, the court enters a plea of not guilty on his or her behalf. In that case, the charges will be set for trial just as if the person standing mute had actually pleaded not guilty instead.

J. TENTH STEP: PRETRIAL MOTIONS

Prior to trial, the prosecutor or defense counsel may file various motions with the court. Such so-called "motion practice" is not as common in criminal proceedings as it is in civil litigation. Nonetheless, one motion in particular is quite common and is extremely important as well: the motion to suppress.

Evidence that has been seized unconstitutionally by law enforcement officers is inadmissible in the prosecutor's case-in-chief against a defendant. While this so-called "exclusionary rule" is subject to numerous exceptions in application, its impact is dramatic in many criminal cases, resulting in the suppression of incriminating evidence.

If, for example, the police stop a defendant's car unconstitutionally and they subsequently discover 10 pounds of marijuana hidden in the trunk, the marijuana may be suppressed. The prosecutor cannot introduce it into evidence against that defendant in a criminal trial. As a result, in a situation like that, the suppression motion is "the whole ball game!" This is true in many narcotics possession cases. Without any marijuana to introduce into evidence in this hypothetical case, no possession of marijuana conviction is possible.

But the exclusionary rule does not *automatically* apply to exclude evidence; rather, defense counsel must move to suppress particular evidence. In response, the court then holds a suppression hearing, a mini-trial where defense counsel calls witnesses and introduces evidence to support the motion, and the prosecutor responds through cross examination and/or by calling his or her own witnesses and introducing other evidence to demonstrate the constitutionality of the seizing officers' conduct. If the judge grants the motion, the evidence is suppressed. If the judge denies the motion, the evidence is admissible.

Other pretrial motions that might be made by counsel include

- motions in limine (seeking to determine the judge's evidentiary rulings in advance);
- motions to quash an indictment;
- motions to recuse (disqualify the judge);
- motions for reductions in bail; and
- motions for change of venue.

K. ELEVENTH STEP: TRIAL

Finally!

As you have just seen, a lot goes on before we actually reach the stage of a criminal trial. In fact, most criminal prosecutions never even reach this stage. Cases (and charges) are dismissed. Some defendants enter pretrial diversion programs. Plea negotiations take place. Guilty pleas are entered. In fact, typically no more than 4 percent of felony defendants who have been arraigned on criminal charges actually end up standing trial:[2]

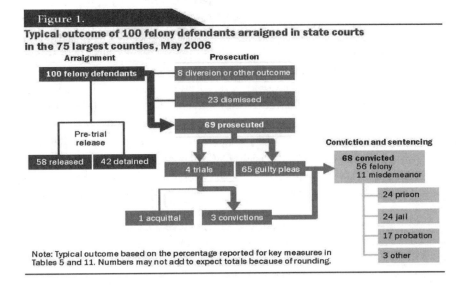

Figure 1.

Typical outcome of 100 felony defendants arraigned in state courts in the 75 largest counties, May 2006

Note: Typical outcome based on the percentage reported for key measures in Tables 5 and 11. Numbers may not add to expect totals because of rounding.

Nonetheless, because the volume of criminal activity and arrests is large, criminal trials still make up a very large percentage of both federal and state trial dockets. Moreover, as a result of the constitutional guarantee of a "speedy trial," in the absence of appropriate waivers, each criminal trial will usually need to take place within 6 months of the filing of criminal charges.

At trial, the prosecutor must prove every element of every charge leveled against a criminal defendant beyond a reasonable doubt. Criminal defendants have a right to a jury in serious criminal cases, i.e., in cases where the defendant could potentially receive a sentence of incarceration in excess of

---

2. Chart and data taken from U.S. Dept. of Justice, Office of Justice Programs, Bureau of Justice Statistics, "Felony Defendants in Large Urban Counties, 2006" (May 2010), http://bjs.ojp.usdoj.gov/content/pub/pdf/fdluc06.pdf.

6 months. Most felony cases are jury trials, and most end with a conviction. The acquittal rate in criminal trials is relatively low at roughly 25 percent.[3]

Once a criminal trial has ended in a conviction, defense counsel often files post-trial motions, usually seeking to set aside the jury's verdict. This motion is rarely granted.

L. TWELFTH STEP: SENTENCING

After a conviction and the preparation of a presentence report, the defendant is subsequently sentenced, usually by the trial judge. Defendants who have been convicted of a capital offense—one that may potentially be subject to the death penalty—are, however, usually sentenced by a jury, either to life in prison or death.

Traditionally, sentencing was indeterminate. That is to say, the legislature established a sentencing range for every crime—sometimes a very wide range (e.g., probation to 20 years in prison)—and the judge exercised his or her discretion to sentence each convicted defendant somewhere within that range. The problem with this approach, in the view of many people, including legislators, is that it led to an extremely wide variation in sentencing patterns. One sentencing judge might sentence a rapist to 20 years in prison, and another sentencing judge in similar circumstances might sentence a rapist to only 6 months.

As a result of concerns about the apparent unfairness arguably inherent in this sort of variation, most legislatures have now adopted determinate sentencing schemes. Determinate sentencing approaches decrease judicial variation in sentencing and increase the likelihood that similarly situated convicted defendants will receive a similar sentence. On the other hand, this result is accomplished by reducing the amount of discretion the sentencing judge has, making it difficult, if not impossible, to tailor a particular sentence to the unique facts of a particular case and the unique characteristics of a particular defendant.

Every jurisdiction has the power to adopt the specific sentencing scheme that it thinks is most appropriate. Some of the most common elements of modern determinate sentencing schemes in the United States include:

- **Guideline sentencing:** This is a system in which every criminal offense is assigned a numerical point score and points are then added or subtracted to that score on the basis of the judge's finding that specified aggravating (e.g., the victim was a child or an elderly person) and mitigating (e.g., the defendant is a first-time offender) factors are present. Depending on the final point total, the judge sentences from

---

3. *Id.*

a range that has been assigned to that specific point total. The federal criminal justice system uses this approach.

- **Flat-time sentencing**: This is a system in which the commission of every crime carries a single, invariable sentence, e.g., a conviction for armed robbery is always punished by 10 years in prison. The sentencing judge has no discretion to diverge from that sentence.
- **Mandatory minimums**: This is a determinate sentencing approach where a defendant convicted of a particular crime or of a particular act in committing a specified crime (e.g., carrying a firearm) must receive a minimum sentence of incarceration of a set amount of time. Although the sentencing judge has discretion as to the upper range of the sentence, he or she has no discretion to diverge from that minimum sentence.

Roughly 70 percent of those defendants who are convicted of felony offenses receive sentences that include a term of incarceration.[4]

M. THIRTEENTH STEP: DIRECT APPEAL

Although there is no federal constitutional right to appeal a criminal conviction, every U.S. jurisdiction has nonetheless established just such a right by law. Usually, the first appeal possible as of right is to an intermediate appellate court. These courts tend to review a very high volume of criminal cases, and their basic task is to apply established law to the facts of numerous cases.

When and if the intermediate appellate court affirms a defendant's conviction (which is what happens most of the time), discretionary appellate review is typically possible by the highest court in the jurisdiction. (Convicted defendants who have been sentenced to death often have *a right* to appellate review in this highest court.) "Discretionary review" means that there is no right to review in that highest appellate court but that the court may decide to review a lower appellate court's decision. Usually, discretionary review of this sort is granted because of the importance or novelty of the issue to be decided or because there has been a conflict in interpretation of the law by different lower courts (or by different panels of the same lower court).

The conviction-reversal rate in appellate courts is quite low, in the range of about 10 to 15 percent in federal courts.[5] If the appellate court reverses the conviction on a question of law, the defendant may then be retried.

---

4. *Id.*
5. *See, e.g., generally* Michael Heise, "Federal Criminal Appeals: A Brief Empirical Perspective," 93 Marq. L. Rev. 825 (2009).

N. FOURTEENTH STEP: POST-CONVICTION REMEDIES

Once a convicted defendant's direct appeal options are exhausted, the conviction is "final." But, even so, he or she may still have an opportunity to raise a further challenge at a later point in so-called "post-conviction" proceedings.

One common form of post-conviction proceeding is a petition for a writ of *habeas corpus*, which can be filed in federal court by a defendant who was convicted in a state court and has exhausted his or her direct appeals. The petitioner seeking *habeas* relief is arguing that the state denied him or her a constitutional right in the state court proceedings. Such petitions are only granted in extraordinary cases.

Similarly, state courts make available different forms of post-conviction relief in situations where extraordinary issues have arisen that were not and could not have been considered in the original appeal process. One of the most common post-conviction claims made by convicted defendants is that their defense counsel did not effectively represent them in the original trial or on direct appeal. Post-conviction relief of this sort, however, just like federal *habeas* petitions, is rarely granted.

O. MISDEMEANORS AND LESSER OFFENSES

The steps set out in this chapter are typical for the adjudication of serious—usually felony—criminal charges. Bear in mind, however, that misdemeanor or lesser charges are often handled with fewer steps and usually result in less serious consequences. Most defendants convicted of misdemeanor offenses are not incarcerated at all. Often, they are simply fined.

CHAPTER 5

Criminal Trials: Judge and Jury

A. FACTS VERSUS LAW: WHO DECIDES WHAT?

Here is the important point to remember: Judges determine the applicable law; juries find facts.

In the early history of the American Colonies and for a time after the Revolution, juries were nearly always recognized as having the power to judge *both* law and fact. But this has changed. Today, in the U.S. legal system, the judge determines the applicable law, and then he or she instructs the jury about the law the jurors should apply to the case before it.

The jury, in turn, using the legal framework given to it by the judge, engages in "fact-finding," i.e., the jurors hear the competing factual accounts presented by the prosecution and the defense and decide what account they believe and whether that account establishes a criminal offense or defense pursuant to the instructional guidelines the judge has given them.

CASE 3. Murder on the high seas: Judges instruct on the law, and juries find the facts. *Sparf and Hansen* is a classic Supreme Court decision that clearly shows the difference in the roles of judge and jury.

The defendants were on trial for murder, and they wanted an instruction that the jury could find them guilty of a lesser offense. But the judge instructed the jury that they could *not* find the defendants guilty of manslaughter or a lesser homicide offense than murder, and the Supreme Court held that the jury could not make its own *legal* determination that such a lesser verdict was appropriate.

SPARF AND HANSEN v. UNITED STATES
156 U.S. 51 (1895).

The Court: Sparf, Hansen and St. Clair were indicted jointly for the murder of Maurice Fitzgerald upon the high seas, on board an American vessel, the bark Hesper. On motion of the accused, it was ordered that they be tried separately. St. Clair was tried, found guilty of murder, and sentenced to suffer the punishment of death. Subsequently the order for separate trials was set aside, and Sparf and Hansen were tried together, and both were convicted of murder. A motion for a new trial having been overruled, a like sentence was imposed upon them.

We are of opinion that the court below did not err in saying to the jury that they could not, consistently with the law arising from the evidence, find the defendants guilty of manslaughter, or of any offense less than the one charged; that if the defendants were not guilty of the offense charged, the duty of the jury was to return a verdict of not guilty. No instruction was given that questioned the right of the jury to determine whether the witnesses were to be believed or not, nor whether the defendant was guilty or not guilty of the offense charged. On the contrary, the court was careful to say that the jury were the exclusive judges of the facts, and that they were to determine—applying to the facts the principles of law announced by the court—whether the evidence established the guilt or innocence of the defendants of the charge set out in the indictment.

The trial was thus conducted upon the theory that it was the duty of the court to expound the law, and that of the jury to apply the law as thus declared to the facts as ascertained by them. In this separation of the functions of court and jury is found the chief value, as well as safety, of the jury system. Those functions cannot be confounded or disregarded without endangering the stability of public justice, as well as the security of private and personal rights.

ANALYSIS

This Nineteenth Century Supreme Court decision makes clear the basic point that judges decide what the law is and instruct the members of the jury accordingly. The jurors' job, in turn, is simply fact-finding, i.e., application of the law to the evidence introduced at trial.

The jury couldn't decide to convict the defendants of manslaughter when the trial judge only charged them on the criminal offense of murder. Guilty or not guilty of murder. That was the jury's job. Its only job.

B. JURY TRIAL WAIVER: BENCH TRIALS

Sometimes, criminal defendants waive their right to a jury trial and elect to be tried by a judge instead. This is called a "bench trial."

So why would an accused person, *any* accused person, waive a jury?

Normally, trying a case to a jury rather than to a judge is viewed as advantageous to a criminal defendant . . . for a number of different reasons. Most significantly, in most states, the jury in a criminal case must reach its verdict unanimously in order to convict. As a result, if defense counsel can convince only a single juror (or more, of course) not to vote to convict, no conviction can be obtained.

When jurors can't agree on a verdict, by the way, the jury is said to be a "hung jury." When a jury has been hung, the prosecution has the right—but not the obligation—to bring the same charges once again in a new trial with a new and different jury.

But there are occasions when it may be advantageous for an accused person to choose to be tried by a judge rather than by a jury. One of the most common situations of this sort is when the facts alleged are so gruesome and the alleged criminal conduct so heinous that defense counsel fears that a lay jury would be predisposed against the accused as an emotional matter. This is often the case in a child sexual abuse prosecution. Or where the victim was tortured. Or where the defendant has been accused of committing mass murders.

Heightened emotions arising out of these horrific facts might cause a juror to focus more on the crime that was committed rather than upon who committed it. Judges, it is argued, are better situated and trained to view these sorts of emotional facts and allegations more dispassionately and fairly. Or, at least that's what some defense counsel believe.

C. JURY NULLIFICATION

In applying the facts to the law, juries sometimes end up ignoring the law. This is called "jury nullification." And it is perfectly lawful. In fact, it is an inevitable part of the way our criminal justice system operates.

CASE 4. Napalming Draft Board files: Juries do not have to follow the judge's instructions. Juries don't have to—and they don't—tell us *why* they have reached a particular verdict. They just tell us what their verdict is. As a result, in that sense, we never know for sure whether each and every one of the jurors has actually followed—or ignored—the judge's instructions.

The federal Fourth Circuit Court of Appeals concluded in *Moylan* that that is simply not a problem. In that case—which was widely publicized and

followed because it was part of a vast anti-war movement in the United States protesting our involvement in Vietnam—the court held that juries do indeed have the right to ignore the law. That's exactly what defense counsel wanted the jury to do, namely, to acquit these obviously guilty defendants—popularly called the "Catonsville 9," all anti-war Catholic activists—*not* because they were innocent, but as part of a protest against the Vietnam War.

Defense counsel "won the battle, but lost the war" on appeal. The Fourth Circuit did uphold the right to jury nullification. But it also concluded that defense counsel could not tell the jurors that they had a right to not follow the law!

UNITED STATES v. MARY MOYLAN, PHILIP BERRIGAN, THOMAS LEWIS, GEORGE J. MISCHE, THOMAS MELVILLE, MARJORIE MELVILLE, JOHN HOGAN, JAMES DARST, AND DANIEL BERRIGAN
417 F.2d 1002 (4th Cir. 1969).

The Court: The defendants appeal their conviction for violation of three federal statutes proscribing the mutilation of Government records, destruction of Government property, and interference with the administration of the Selective Service System. The facts are uncontroverted. At 12:50 P.M. on May 17, 1968, the appellants entered the office of Local Board No. 33 in Catonsville, Maryland, and removed approximately 378 files to an adjacent parking lot where they burned the files with home-made napalm. The defendants, men and women with sincere and strong commitments, readily admit the commission of these acts as a protest against the war in Vietnam.

Defendants contend that the trial judge should have informed the jury, as requested, that it had the power to acquit even if appellants were clearly guilty of the charged offenses. They maintain that the judge should have told the jury this or permitted their counsel to argue it to the jury in the face of the judge's instruction on the law. Defendants reason that since the jury has "the power to bring in a verdict in the teeth of both law and facts," then the jury should be told that it has this power. Furthermore, the argument runs, the jury's power to acquit where the law may dictate otherwise is a fundamental necessity of a democratic system. Only in this way, it is said, can a man's actions be judged fairly by society speaking through the jury, or a law which is considered too harsh be mitigated.

We recognize, as defendants urge, the undisputed power of the jury to acquit, even if its verdict is contrary to the law as given by the judge and contrary to the evidence. This is a power that must exist as long as we adhere to the general verdict in criminal cases, for the courts cannot search the minds of the jurors to find the basis upon which they judge. If the jury feels that the law under which the defendant is accused is unjust, or that exigent circumstances justified the actions of the accused, or for any reason which appeals to their logic or passion, the jury has the power to acquit, and the courts must abide by that decision.

Concededly, this power of the jury is not always contrary to the interests of justice. For example, freedom of the press was immeasurably strengthened by the jury's acquittal of John Peter Zenger of seditious libel, a violation of which, under the law as it then existed and the facts, he was clearly guilty. In that case Andrew Hamilton was allowed to urge the jury, in the face of the judge's charge, "to see with their own eyes, to hear with their own ears, and to make use of their consciences and understanding in judging of the lives, liberties, or estates of their fellow subjects."

No less an authority than the eminent, late Dean Roscoe Pound of Harvard Law School has expressed the opinion that "Jury lawlessness is the great corrective of law in its actual administration." However, this is not to say that the jury should be encouraged in their "lawlessness," and by clearly stating to the jury that they may disregard the law, telling them that they may decide according to their prejudices or consciences (for there is no check to insure that the judgment is based upon con- science rather than prejudice), we would indeed be negating the rule of law in favor of the rule of lawlessness. This should not be allowed.

To encourage individuals to make their own determinations as to which laws they will obey and which they will permit themselves as a matter of conscience to disobey is to invite chaos. No legal system could long survive if it gave every individual the option of disregarding with impunity any law which by his personal standard was judged morally untenable. Toleration of such conduct would not be democratic, as defendants claim, but inevitably anarchic.

ANALYSIS

The court concluded that the jury *must* have the power to ignore the law as long as the general verdict is used in criminal cases. What is a "general verdict?" It's a jury verdict of guilty or not guilty, with no further elucidation or explanation of the jurors' rationale for their decision.

But, the court added, even though juries can ignore the law, they shouldn't be encouraged to do so. So they can do it; they just can't be told that they can do it.

The sentences of the Catonsville 9 defendants were, as a result, upheld. The most prominent member of the group, Father Phillip Berrigan, was sentenced to 3 ½ years of imprisonment. He disappeared and was a fugitive for a time, but was ultimately found by the FBI and served his time in federal prison.

D. CRIMINAL TRIAL NARRATIVES

One of the implications of the possibility of jury nullification in our criminal justice system is that lawyers, criminal defense counsel, *and* prosecutors will often attempt to influence jurors to focus on something other than the elements of criminal offenses and defenses that they are instructed to focus upon by the trial judge because they know that juries can ignore the law. The lawyers can't do this openly and expressly because, as the *Moylan* decision set out above makes clear, even though juries can ignore the law, they can't be encouraged to do it. But that doesn't mean jury nullification won't happen. It does.

A criminal defense attorney might, for example, try to get the jury to consider and sympathize with his or her client's terrible, abusive upbringing, the extenuating circumstances the accused was facing, the failings of the alleged victim, or the brutality of the police in arresting him. A prosecutor, in contrast, might want the jurors to consider and sympathize with the victim's suffering and that of the victim's family, the antisocial personality of the accused, or the criminal nature of his or her associates or associations.

Look, our criminal justice system isn't perfect. The theory and the reality of criminal trials sometimes—actually, quite often—diverge, sometimes substantially.

You can't understand the true nature of what takes place in criminal trials in this country until you consider the fact that in addition to the prosecution trying to establish all of the elements of the charged crimes and the defense trying to defend against those charges, both sides are often also trying to present to the jury—albeit indirectly—their own emotive narrative—a "story"—about just why the accused should be convicted . . . or not.

Jurors often pay attention to these stories and sometimes render their judgments on that basis by convicting, acquitting, or mitigating the severity of the offense. When you understand that, you have a much more realistic understanding of what is actually going on in criminal trials.

E. CIVIL DISOBEDIENCE AND JURY NULLIFICATION

The anti-war defendants in the *Moylan* case were trying to get the jury to nullify their criminal acts by persuading the jury or, at least one of the jurors, to sympathize with their pacifistic point of view and to vote accordingly. They knew that they were violating the law, but they hoped that the jury would ignore that violation in sympathy with their motivation for acting.

In our justice system, people are obligated to follow the law even when it runs contrary to their moral, political, religious, or ideological beliefs. Nonetheless, some people feel so strongly about one issue or another that they choose not to follow the law. Absent jury nullification, such "civil disobedience" is not a defense to criminal activity.

F. JUDICIAL RULINGS "AS A MATTER OF LAW"

Although, as previously discussed, judges determine the law and juries find the facts (except in bench trials), there are nonetheless some occasions where judges rule on the facts . . . *as a matter of law*.

What does that mean?

It means that a judge may decide *as a matter of law* that the prosecution has not put into evidence enough facts to support a jury verdict on a particular charge. This is not a factual ruling; rather, it's a legal ruling (i.e., there were not enough facts in evidence as a legal matter).

Moreover, even *after* a jury has returned a Guilty verdict on a particular charge, the trial judge may nonetheless direct a verdict for the defendant on that charge if the judge finds that no reasonable jury could have convicted on the basis of the facts in the record. However, a judge may not direct a verdict for the State no matter how overwhelming the evidence. Once the jury has reached a verdict of acquittal, that's the end of the matter.

Nonetheless, a trial judge may decide that an accused criminal defendant is *not* entitled to an instruction about a potential defense to conviction because the defense has not put into evidence enough facts to support a jury verdict on that defense.

For example, a trial judge may decide that a defendant who is defending against a first-degree murder charge is not entitled to an instruction on voluntary manslaughter, a lesser offense. The judge might rule that way because he or she has concluded that the defense did not introduce enough evidence to support a reasonable jury's conclusion that the defendant was adequately provoked to kill, a necessary finding in order to entitle a defendant to a lesser verdict of voluntary manslaughter in most jurisdictions.

G. CONSTITUTIONAL ISSUES: ROLE OF THE JURY

There are some significant constitutional issues relevant to the difference in the judge and the jury's role in a criminal trial.

For example and importantly, the Sixth Amendment to the U.S. Constitution provides, *inter alia*, that criminal defendants have a right to a jury trial. Supreme Court decisions have further established that that jury-trial right applies to all serious criminal cases, cases where a convicted defendant could be potentially sentenced to more than 6 months in prison.

Moreover, the Supreme Court has ruled that the Fourteenth Amendment requires that the prosecution bear the burden of proving each fact necessary to establish an element of a charged offense beyond a reasonable doubt. If the defense can create a reasonable doubt as to any one of those elements in the minds of the jury, it must acquit the accused of that charge. *See* further discussion of the significance of this point in the next chapter, Chapter 6.

Finally and significantly, the Supreme Court has also ruled that when a defendant is tried by a jury, any fact necessary to support a sentence exceeding the maximum authorized by law—other than the fact of a prior conviction—must either be admitted by the defendant or proved to the jury beyond a reasonable doubt.

CASE 5. Crack cocaine and the sentencing guidelines: Juries decide how much crack cocaine there is for sentencing purposes, not the judge. The *Booker* decision is a very important case. It made it crystal clear that the jury—*not the judge*—must find any fact necessary to support a sentence exceeding the maximum authorized by law beyond a reasonable doubt.

In *Booker*, the precise amount of cocaine in the possession of a defendant was a key fact. The amount was important because the potential sentence varied with the amount of cocaine; the more cocaine, the higher the sentence. The issue on appeal was whether the judge erred when the judge sentenced Booker to a longer prison term based on the judge's own fact finding made by a preponderance of the evidence—after the jury verdict—as to the amount of cocaine Booker possessed. Because the judge made that factual determination rather than letting the jury do it, Booker's sentence was reversed.

UNITED STATES v. FREDDIE J. BOOKER

543 U.S. 220 (2005).

The Court: The question presented is whether an application of the Federal Sentencing Guidelines violated the Sixth Amendment. In each case, the courts below held that binding rules set forth in the Guidelines limited the severity of the sentence that the judge could lawfully impose on the defendant based on the facts found by the jury at his trial.

Booker was charged with possession with intent to distribute at least 50 grams of cocaine base (crack). Having heard evidence that he had 92.5 grams in his duffel bag, the jury found him guilty of violating 21 U.S.C. §841(a)(1). That statute prescribes a minimum sentence of 10 years in prison and a maximum sentence of life for that offense.

Based upon Booker's criminal history and the quantity of drugs found by the jury, the Sentencing Guidelines required the District Court Judge to select a "base" sentence of not less than 210 or more than 262 months in prison. The judge, however, held a post-trial sentencing proceeding and concluded by a preponderance of the evidence that Booker had possessed an additional 566 grams of crack and that he was guilty of obstructing justice. Those findings mandated that the judge select a sentence between 360 months and life imprisonment; the judge imposed a sentence at the low end of the range. Thus, instead of the sentence of 21 years and 10 months that the judge could have imposed on the basis of the facts proved to the jury beyond a reasonable doubt, Booker received a 30-year sentence.

It has been settled throughout our history that the Constitution protects every criminal defendant "against conviction except upon proof beyond a reasonable doubt of every fact necessary to constitute the crime with which he is charged." It is equally clear that the "Constitution gives a criminal defendant the right to demand that a jury find him guilty of all the elements of the crime with which he is charged."

Booker's actual sentence was 360 months, almost 10 years longer than the Guidelines range supported by the jury verdict alone. To reach this sentence, the judge found facts beyond those found by the jury: namely, that Booker possessed 566 grams of crack in addition to the 92.5 grams in his duffel bag. The jury never heard any evidence of the additional drug quantity, and the judge found it true by a preponderance of the evidence. Thus, the jury's verdict alone does not authorize the sentence. The judge acquires that authority only upon finding some additional fact.

> Any fact (other than a prior conviction) which is necessary to support a sentence exceeding the maximum authorized by the facts established by a plea of guilty or a jury verdict must be admitted by the defendant or proved to a jury beyond a reasonable doubt.

ANALYSIS

The problem here was that the judge found a significant fact, not the jury. Fact-finding is the jury's province, not the trial judge's role. While judges have discretion to consider numerous facts and factors in sentencing a convicted defendant *within the sentencing range set by the Legislature*, the Supreme Court stressed that judges cannot engage in their own fact-finding in order to sentence above that range.

That doesn't mean that Booker couldn't have lawfully received that higher sentence. If the same jury that convicted Booker of intent to distribute cocaine had also been asked to, and subsequently did, find beyond a reasonable doubt that he had possessed that additional 566 grams of crack, thus permitting a higher sentence under the federal Sentencing Guidelines, that procedure would have been just fine. But, the point is, a sentencing judge couldn't do that. Again, the jury, not the judge, finds the facts.

Booker's case was remanded to the lower court for resentencing.

CHAPTER 6

Statutory Element Analysis: The Way Criminal Law Works

A. THE IMPORTANCE OF ELEMENT ANALYSIS

One of the most important keys to understanding just how criminal trials work, how Criminal Law is applied in the United States, and to understanding what is really going on when you read appellate decisions in criminal cases is to understand the concept of "element analysis."

Remember, as noted in Chapter 5, the Supreme Court ruled that the Fourteenth Amendment requires that the prosecution bear the burden of proving each fact necessary to establish an *element* of a charged offense beyond a reasonable doubt. If the defense can create a reasonable doubt as to any one of those elements in the minds of the jury, it must acquit the accused of that charge.

So what exactly are these elements to which the Supreme Court is referring? And why are they so important? Glad you asked.

The focus upon element analysis is a product of the widespread adoption after 1962 of ALI's MPC approach to defining criminal offenses and defenses. *See* further discussion of the MPC in Chapter 8. Under the MPC, each criminal offense and defense is broken down into a set of elements—that is, specified facts that needed to be proved in order to establish the defendant's culpability or innocence. These elements relate to

- the defendant's conduct;
- the attendant circumstances surrounding the event; or
- the result of the defendant's conduct.

Once you add in the Supreme Court's Fourteenth Amendment rulings that we have already talked about, the result is that criminal trials in this country consist of the prosecution's effort to establish each element of each charged crime beyond a reasonable doubt. Defense counsel, in contrast, tries either to "negative" one or more of the elements of each charged offense (by creating a reasonable doubt) or to prove an "affirmative defense" in order to successfully defend his or her client. (Defending a criminal defendant by "negativing" an element or proving an affirmative defense is discussed further in Chapter 7.)

However, breaking a criminal statute down into its requisite elements is sometimes more art than science. And some elements have subelements, too. This point is probably best illustrated by giving you an example.

Consider Pennsylvania's indecent exposure statute, 18 Pa.C.S.A. §3127(a). That statute provides as follows:

> A person commits indecent exposure if that person exposes his or her genitals in any public place or in any place where there are present other persons under circumstances in which he or she knows or should know that this conduct is likely to offend, affront or alarm.

So what does a prosecutor have to prove in order to convict someone of indecent exposure in Pennsylvania? Well, a natural (but not the only) way to parse the elements in this statute would be as follows:

The prosecutor would have to prove each and every one of these elements . . . beyond a reasonable doubt:

That the accused

(1) exposed
(2) his or her genitals
(3) (a) in any public place
      or
   (b) in any place where there are present other persons
(4) under circumstances in which he or she
   (a) knows
      or
   (b) should know
(5) that this conduct is likely to
   (a) offend,
   (b) affront,
      or
   (c) alarm.

All defense counsel would have to do to gain an acquittal on an indecent exposure charge in Pennsylvania would be to create a reasonable doubt in the minds of the jury as to any one or more of these elements. If defense counsel does that, the jury must acquit.

And note that the outline of elements set out above is not the only way you could have envisioned these elements. For example, some people would argue that the word "likely" in Element 5 should be its own separate element. If defense counsel convinced a jury that it was only "possible" (not "likely," as the statute requires) that an act of exposure would offend, affront, or alarm someone, then the prosecution would not have met its burden of proof.

So what if a woman is arrested and charged with indecent exposure under this statute for sunbathing topless on her back patio? Well, the answer is *that this is not the crime of indecent exposure.* The prosecutor can't prove Element 2 beyond a reasonable doubt, namely that this woman exposed her genitals. Genitals are reproductive organs. Breasts are not genitals.

Indeed, even if the Pennsylvania legislature had expressly included the exposure of female breasts in addition to genitals in this statute (which it could do), there is every chance that depending on the additional facts and circumstances present, defense counsel would still be successful in defending this accused woman. With respect to Element 3, for example, was her patio a public place or a place where other persons were present? If not—or, more accurately, if defense counsel can establish a reasonable doubt about that element—she would not be found to be guilty of indecent exposure.

Moreover, with respect to Elements 4 and 5, were the circumstances such that this accused woman knew or should have known that her conduct was likely to offend, affront, or alarm other people? If not or if there is simply a reasonable doubt about that element, again, she could not be found to be guilty of indecent exposure. There is, of course, every chance that a woman sunbathing topless on her own patio might well have thought that she wouldn't be seen by others who would be upset by that. Change the venue from her patio to a beach full of nude sunbathers, and that would almost certainly be the case.

Be careful now about what you learn from this type of element analysis. This hypothetical topless sunbathing, based upon a real statute, does *not* mean that topless sunbathing by females is necessarily lawful in Pennsylvania. All it means is that, in these circumstances, it is not a criminal offense *under this statute.*

There may be another criminal statute that applies to this conduct. (And, in fact, there is.) And there may be a separate Pennsylvania statute that provides that a mother cannot be convicted in any case for exposing her breast while nursing her child. (This also is the case.) You must be careful to analyze the application of each and every criminal statute separately. One statute may not cover conduct that is instead covered by another statute.

Consider another hypothetical situation under this same statute: It's late one night. The bars have just closed. One of the young men leaving a bar with his friends dashes into a nearby alley and urinates against the wall. He is seen by a group of young women passing by the alley on the sidewalk who shriek, laugh, and point at him, and then run off. What's this (aside from gross, unhygienic, rude, tacky, immature, and vulgar)? Is it indecent exposure under the statute set out above?

Don't read on just yet!

Stop and apply the law to these facts. Can the prosecution prove each and every one of the statutory elements in this situation beyond a reasonable doubt? Can defense counsel raise a reasonable doubt about any one or more of them?

Okay, are you ready? Have you tried it yourself?

Did you notice that Elements 1 and 2 seem clear in this scenario? This guy clearly exposed his genitals, didn't he?

What about Element 3, though? Was this alley public or private? Or was it a "place where there [were] present other persons"? It's certainly possible that no one else was actually in the alley. The women who saw him weren't in the alley. They were on the sidewalk. Remember, defense counsel doesn't have to prove that no one was present. All defense counsel has to do is to raise a reasonable doubt in the minds of the jury.

Of course, the likely focus of the defense in this hypothetical scenario will center on Elements 4 and 5, right? Did this episode take place under circumstances where the accused urinator knew or should have known that his conduct was likely to offend, affront, or alarm anyone? Can the prosecutor prove each one of those elements, however many you see there, beyond a reasonable doubt? Of course, in real life, that's a question for the jury.

What types of reasonable doubt would you as defense counsel try to establish? Wouldn't you argue that he went into that alley precisely because he didn't want to be seen? *Should* he have known better? Were there hordes of people around? Or was the area abutting the alley virtually deserted? Did he know or should he have known that someone was likely to be offended, affronted, or alarmed? If defense counsel can find one (or more) of the young women who saw him and she testifies that she wasn't offended, affronted, or alarmed, but rather was amused (which is why they laughed and pointed at him), would that necessarily win his case for him? What if the prosecutor put her on the stand instead and she testified that: "Ewww. I have never been so grossed out in my whole life." Does that establish Elements 4 and 5 beyond a reasonable doubt?

You see? This is what criminal trials are like. The prosecution presents all the testimony and evidence it can come up with in order to establish each and every element of every charged offense, and the defense tries to raise a reasonable doubt in the minds of the jury about the existence of as many of those elements as possible.

This also should explain a lot about what criminal appeals often focus upon, namely did the prosecution introduce enough evidence to establish each element of a convicted offense?

CASE 6. Taking the '57 Chevy from the showroom window: Every element of the criminal offense, including the requisite criminal intent, must be established in order to support a conviction. Louis Henderson Branch shattered the showroom window with a concrete block, climbed inside, and drove off with a car. You would think that this conduct would easily make out the crime of theft, right?

THE BURGLARY OF THE COOL CAR

Nope. Think again. As the Iowa Court of Appeals explains, the prosecution simply failed to establish one of the elements of the theft crime charged—the requisite mens rea. When that is the case (that is, when one or more elements of the criminal offense is not proved beyond a reasonable doubt), then the criminal conviction cannot stand. The theft conviction was, accordingly, reversed.

specific criminal intent

But . . . please do not read this case as a license to steal! Branch's burglary conviction was affirmed. Why? Because all the elements of that separate criminal offense were established beyond a reasonable doubt by the prosecution.

STATE OF IOWA v. LOUIS HENDERSON BRANCH
810 N.W.2d 25 (Iowa Ct. App. 2011).

The Court: Shortly before midnight on March 16, 2009, an intoxicated Branch was walking along Locust Street in downtown Des Moines. He wandered to American Dream Machines, a car dealership specializing in classic cars, located at 1500 Locust. The dealership was closed, and Branch stood outside looking at the cars in the showroom through the dealership windows. He picked up a concrete rock and threw it at the windows. After several attempts, Branch managed to break a window and enter the dealership. Branch was able to start the ignition of a 1957 Chevrolet Bel Air that was on display. He drove the vehicle out of the building through a closed glass garage door, sounding an alarm.

Branch argues the record does not contain substantial evidence to support his convictions for theft in the first degree and burglary in the third degree. The offense of theft has two elements. A person commits theft when he (1) takes possession or control of the property of another, or property in the possession of another (2) with the intent to permanently deprive the other thereof. Iowa Code §714.1(1). We acknowledge section 714.1 requires only an intent to deprive the owner of his or her property; however, our supreme court has interpreted section 714.1 to require "an intent to permanently deprive the owner of his property."

Proof the defendant acted with the purpose to permanently deprive an owner of property requires a determination of what the defendant was thinking when an act was done. When determining criminal intent, the condition of the mind at the time the crime is committed is rarely susceptible of direct proof but depends on many factors. Specific intent may be inferred from the facts and circumstances surrounding the act, as well as any reasonable inferences to be drawn from those facts and circumstances.

In this case, an intoxicated Branch took a vehicle from American Dream Machines without permission. The mere fact Branch took the vehicle without consent does not give rise to an inference he intended to permanently deprive American Dream Machines of the vehicle. Branch drove through a glass garage door and began driving the wrong direction down a one-way street. Branch did not cause damage to the vehicle with any admitted purpose or apparent plan to destruct the vehicle. In essence, damage alone, without other circumstantial evidence reflecting an intent to damage the vehicle to deprive the owner of the vehicle is not enough.

Further, there were no admissions by Branch or statements from other witnesses that would indicate his "purpose in taking the vehicle." Indeed, Branch's sister testified Branch was an alcoholic who suffered from blackouts and she and other family members had to take care of him. She stated he had been drinking all day long prior to the evening he took the vehicle. Branch testified he did not remember anything after he went for a walk and the next thing he knew, he was waking up in Polk County Jail detox. He further stated he had not driven a car in years and had not intended to take a vehicle. Although the jury was free to reject the testimony of Branch and his sister as not credible, there is little other evidence by which to judge Branch's state of mind at the time he took the vehicle.

Under these circumstances, the record does not reveal substantial evidence to support a finding Branch intended to permanently deprive the owner of the property. Accordingly, we find there was insufficient evidence to support a conviction under section 714.2(1).

In conjunction with his insufficiency of the evidence claim to support his conviction for theft, Branch argues that "[b]ecause the State failed to present sufficient evidence [he] had the intent to permanently deprive the owner of the vehicle, i.e., the intent to commit a theft, the State also did not prove the crime of third-degree burglary." Indeed, the offense of burglary requires the State to prove, in part, that "the defendant broke and/or entered . . . with the intent to commit a theft." However, a defendant may have the intent to commit a theft at the time he broke or entered the building, but subsequently forgo that intent at the time he took possession or control of the vehicle. Here, the evidence is undisputed that Branch broke into the American Dream Machines business, a place where valuable vehicles were stored, by picking up a concrete rock and breaking a window. Accordingly, [nothing precludes] the jury's determination that Branch committed burglary in the third degree, and his claim in regard to his burglary conviction must fail.

ANALYSIS

Branch's conviction of theft in the first degree had to be reversed because the prosecution did not establish one of the elements of that criminal offense beyond a reasonable doubt. Under the Iowa statutory language, as interpreted by the Iowa Supreme Court, the prosecution had to establish Branch's intent to *permanently* deprive the car dealership of this 1957 Chevy. But the prosecution presented insufficient evidence to prove that required element of the offense.

However, the court did uphold Branch's conviction for burglary in the third degree. Even though one of the elements of that crime requires proof of the "intent to commit a theft," the fact that the court had concluded that Branch did not in fact commit a theft did not mean that the jury could not have found on the evidence before them that he *intended* to commit a theft. In fact, the jury—the fact-finder—found just that, that he intended to commit a theft when he broke the showroom window. Accordingly and appropriately, the court affirmed that particular conviction.

CASE 7. The high school bully: Every element of the criminal offense, including the status of the victim, must be established in order to support a conviction. Once again, the facts on their face seem pretty clear. J. S. R. (criminal cases involving juveniles use only the accused juvenile's initials, not their names) threatened the Vice-Principal after the Vice-Principal took away his iPod. You would think that this conduct would easily make out the crime of retaliation in Texas, right?

But you've probably already learned by now not to rush to judgment on this type of conclusion, haven't you?

To successfully establish any charged crime, the prosecution must prove *every* single element of the crime that it has charged beyond a reasonable doubt. Once again, as in the preceding Branch case, the prosecution failed to do that. Or so the Texas Court of Appeals held. The prosecution charged J. S. R. with retaliating because of the Vice-Principal's "status." But, the court ruled that the prosecution didn't prove precisely that; it didn't prove that the defendant threatened to harm the Vice-Principal simply *because of his status as Vice-Principal*.

The result? Conviction reversed.

juvinile

IN THE MATTER OF J. S. R., a Child
2011 WL 6183571 (Tex. Ct. App.-Amarillo 2011).

The Court: The juvenile court of Moore County adjudicated appellant J.S.R. delinquent for committing the offense of retaliation and committed him to the custody of the Texas Youth Commission for an indeterminate period not beyond his nineteenth birthday. On appeal, J.S.R. challenges the sufficiency of the evidence.

In its petition, the State alleged: On or about the 20th day of October, 2010 [J.S.R.] did then and there, in the County of Moore, State of Texas, intentionally or knowingly threaten to harm another, Rob Groves, by an unlawful act, to-wit: threaten bodily harm, in retaliation for or on account of the status of Rob Groves as Assistant Principal of Dumas High School suspending said [J.S.R.] from school for misconduct.

At the adjudication hearing, the State's evidence was developed largely through the testimony of Mr. Groves. On October 20, 2010, he decided to suspend J.S.R. from school for a classroom discipline matter, apparently involving J.S.R.'s iPod mp3 player. The iPod was taken from J.S.R. and delivered to Groves. J.S.R. was then brought to Groves' office and the suspension paperwork was signed. Groves agreed that J.S.R. seemed "fine" with the suspension. But when his mother told J.S.R. the school would keep his iPod, he shoved his chair, stood up, and declared, "that's f'd up." Groves responded that such language was not allowed in his office. J.S.R. replied he was not "f-ing scared" of Groves. Groves summoned a school police officer. J.S.R. removed his coat, threw it on the floor and moved toward Groves at his desk. The officer entered the office and stepped between Groves and J.S.R. J.S.R. then told Groves he would catch him "on the street somewhere and f'k [him] up."

The Court of Criminal Appeals has described Penal Code §36.06, "Obstruction or Retaliation" as "a good example of the 'Chinese Menu' style of alleging the elements of a penal offense." Several of the elements present alternatives for charging the offense. The elements and alternatives of the offense are:

(1) The Defendant
(2) a. intentionally [or]
    b. knowingly
(3) a. harms [or]
    b. threatens to harm
(4) another person
(5) by an unlawful act
(6) a. in retaliation for [or]
    b. on account of
(7) a. the service of another [or]
    b. the status of another
(8) as a
    a. public servant
    b. witness
    c. prospective witness [or]
    d. informant.

elements of §36.06

The State's charging instrument must allege at least one item from each numbered elemental category.

The State limited its proof options at the adjudication hearing by alleging only that J.S.R. acted in retaliation for Groves' status. The record shows Groves suspended J.S.R. from school as part of Groves' service as associate principal. During the suspension procedure, he threatened to harm Groves by an unlawful act, because Groves kept his iPod or because Groves summoned school police. But no evidence shows the threatened retaliation was because of GroveS' status as associate principal. Because the State did not present any evidence that the threatened retaliatory conduct was on account of Groves' status as associate principal, it did not prove each element of the charged offense beyond a reasonable doubt. We reverse the judgment of the trial court and render a judgment of acquittal.

ANALYSIS

J. S. R.'s conviction was reversed because the prosecution failed to establish one of the elements of the charged crime—that J. S. R. made his threat in retaliation for Groves' status—*see* Element 7(b) above—beyond a reasonable doubt.

How could the prosecution have *successfully* established this element of the crime of retaliation? Any number of ways. By showing, for example, that J. S. R. had added, as he made his threat, a reference on the order of "No principal is going to mess with me," or something like that. Of course, the prosecution doesn't get to make up any facts it likes in order to suit its prosecution. It needs to do precisely the opposite in fact—prosecutors should bring charges that fit the facts. If there was no indication that J. S. R. made his threat due to Groves' status, this was simply the wrong criminal charge to bring against J. S. R.

B. HOW ELEMENT ANALYSIS AFFECTS CRIMINAL TRIALS

Because proof of each of the elements of a charged crime beyond a reasonable doubt is the prosecutor's obligation and raising a reasonable doubt about one or more of those elements is defense counsel's task (at least where the facts support such a defense), criminal trials for the "same" offense can be *very* different from state to state, depending on the variations in the specific elements of the crime in each state.

Consider, for example, the following rape statutes from three different states:

Utah §76-5-402(1): A person commits rape when the actor has sexual intercourse with another person without the victim's consent.

Indiana §35-42-4-1(a)(1): [A] person who knowingly or intentionally has sexual intercourse with a member of the opposite sex when . . . the other person is compelled by force or imminent threat of force commits rape[.]

Hawaii §707-730(1)(a): A person commits the offense of sexual assault in the first degree if [t]he person knowingly subjects another person to an act of sexual penetration by strong compulsion.

Each of these statutes describes the crime of rape (termed "sexual assault in the first degree" in Hawaii, the highest level of sexual assault) in its jurisdiction. But each of these statutes is quite different in approach. In fact, each statute contains one or more elements that is (are) different from the other states. Once again, whichever state is prosecuting an accused for the crime of rape, the prosecution has to establish each of the relevant elements beyond a reasonable doubt and defense counsel can defend by raising a reasonable doubt as to one or more of those elements.

Let's break down the statutes set out above according to their different elements. In Utah, to convict a defendant—let's just call him X—of the crime of rape, the prosecutor would have to prove beyond a reasonable doubt that the defendant:

(1) Had sexual intercourse
(2) with another person
(3) without the victim's consent.

In Indiana, in contrast, to convict X of rape, the prosecutor would have to prove beyond a reasonable doubt that the defendant

(1) (a) knowingly ⎱ *mens rea*
      or
   (b) intentionally ⎰
(2) had sexual intercourse
(3) with a member of the opposite sex
(4) when . . . the other person is compelled by
   (a) force
      or
   (b)(i)   imminent ← *"if you don't have sex w/ me someday I'll hurt you"*
      (ii)   threat of force.

And finally, in Hawaii, to convict X of rape, the prosecutor would have to prove beyond a reasonable doubt that the defendant

(1) knowingly
(2) subjected another person
(3) to an act of sexual penetration
(4) by
   (a) strong
   (b) compulsion.

Look how differently each of these three states has defined the crime of rape. This is true, by the way, of virtually *every* state, not just these three. In almost every state, the crime of rape is defined differently, although sometimes the differences are very minor.

There is, of course, no legal or constitutional problem with this difference in approach. Each sovereign state has the lawful authority and right to make the *political* decision to criminalize rape—or any other offense—in whatever way it desires. *See* Chapter 8 for additional discussion of this point.

For the purposes of the discussion in this chapter, however, it is important to note that—on the very same sexual assault facts—prosecutors in Utah, Indiana, and Hawaii would have to prove some very different elements beyond a reasonable doubt in order to successfully convict X of rape. And even more significant perhaps, defense counsel in these different jurisdictions would be defending these cases very, very differently . . . *even though the facts are exactly the same.*

For example, one way to defend against an accusation of rape in the state of Utah is to raise a reasonable doubt about whether the supposed victim of the assault actually consented to intercourse. *See* Utah Element 3. A defense like that would very likely focus much of the trial defense on the victim and his or her behavior, i.e., did he or she *really* consent—or not—to sexual intercourse?

But that wouldn't or shouldn't happen to the same extent in Indiana or Hawaii, where the victim's lack of consent is not an element of the offense. (By the way, there are strict evidentiary limits in most states on what kinds of questioning and evidence relating to the victim is admissible in a rape prosecution. Under so-called "rape shield laws," defense counsel is generally not permitted, for example, to question a rape victim—or introduce evidence—about his or her prior sexual experiences.)

In Indiana, unlike Utah, one way to defend against an accusation of rape would be for defense counsel to raise a reasonable doubt about whether the supposed victim of the assault was *actually* compelled by force or the imminent threat of force to engage in sexual intercourse. *See* Indiana Element 4.

A defense like that would very likely focus much of the evidence on the defendant rather than the victim, i.e., did he or she really compel the victim to have sex? If he didn't force *her* to submit to him, did he threaten her with the use of force? (Note the use of single gender pronouns here as rape in Indiana—under this statute at least—*only* applies to victims of the opposite sex; *see* Indiana Element 3.)

And even if the use of force is conceded, defense counsel can still defend a rape prosecution successfully in Indiana by arguing that there is a reasonable doubt that a threat of force was a threat of *imminent* force. That's an issue and a line of defense that would be irrelevant in Utah . . . and in Hawaii.

Imagine how different the defense of X would be in Indiana than in Utah. In Utah, defense counsel might focus on negativing the element of the victim's lack of consent; in Indiana, defense counsel might focus instead on negativing the defendant's use of force or threat of imminent force. The point is, once again, that on the very same facts, these would be very different trials in terms of the evidence introduced and the arguments made to the judge and to the jury.

The same is true of the crime of rape in Hawaii. In Hawaii, "compulsion" of the victim to have sex is an element of the sexual assault offense like Indiana and unlike Utah. *See* Hawaii Element 4(b). But, in Hawaii, unlike Indiana, the prosecutor must prove beyond a reasonable doubt that the compulsion was "strong" in order to obtain a rape conviction. A showing of sexual intercourse induced by a defendant's compulsion alone is not enough. Apparently, "weak compulsion" is not enough to establish the crime of rape!

As a result, unlike both Utah and Indiana, it is easy to imagine rape prosecutions in Hawaii where defense counsel focuses his or her arguments and evidence on creating a reasonable doubt about whether any compulsion to have sex that his or her client exerted was "strong" compulsion. Or not. How very different that trial in Hawaii would be from rape trials in the two other states . . . *and on the very same facts*!

Of course, in analyzing statutory elements of criminal offenses, it is critical that you research any judicial interpretation of the terms of art contained in those elements. If a court with appropriate authority ruled, for example, that *any* forcible compulsion is "strong compulsion" for purposes of this statute, for example, then that is exactly what strong compulsion would mean, even though that is not how the statute reads.

CASE 8. Rape by "strong compulsion" in Hawaii: The elements of the crime dictate the nature of the necessary proofs at trial. Here is an example demonstrating the kinds of proof that have to be established by the prosecution in order to make out the crime of rape by strong compulsion in Hawaii. The Hawaii Supreme Court found the evidence to be overwhelming and affirmed John Veikoso's rape conviction accordingly.

As in the preceding case involving a juvenile identified only by his initials, sexual assault victims are also usually identified by the use of initials or some sort of code (here CW #2).

STATE OF HAWAII v. JOHN C. VEIKOSO
126 Hawai'i 267, 270 P.3d 997 (Hawai'i 2011).

The Court: John Veikoso was charged with two counts of Sexual Assault in the First Degree. As to Count 4, the jury was instructed that the offense of Sexual Assault in the First Degree has three material elements: (1) Veikoso subjected CW # 2 to an act of sexual penetration by inserting his penis into her mouth, (2) by strong compulsion, and (3) did so knowingly as to each element of the offense. As to Count 5, the jury was instructed that the elements of Sexual Assault in the First Degree were: (1) Veikoso subjected CW # 2 to an act of sexual penetration by inserting his penis into her genital opening, (2) by strong compulsion, and (3) did so knowingly as to each element of the offense.

As to the element of "strong compulsion" under both Counts 4 and 5, there was evidence that Veikoso used both "threat[s]," plac[ing] [CW # 2] "in fear of bodily injury" or "in fear that [she would] . . . be kidnapped[,]" and "physical force" "to overcome CW # 2." As to threats, CW # 2 testified that Veikoso repeatedly told her, "Shut the fuck up[,] . . . you're going to do what I tell you to do"; when she started screaming, Veikoso threatened, "Shut the fuck up or I'm going to shoot you"; when Veikoso grabbed CW # 2's hair after she grabbed the handle of Veikoso's vehicle, CW # 2 pulled free and Veikoso said, "Oh, what the fuck are you doing? I'm going to crack you again"; while driving, CW # 2 turned off Veikoso's ignition and Veikoso said, "Look at what the fuck you did, bitch . . . . Oh, you want me to crack you again?"; at some point after she had attempted to escape from his vehicle, Veikoso told CW # 2 that "[t]he last girl that was with [him] got out, but she broke her collarbone"; upon arriving at Maunawili Elementary School, Respondent warned, "[Y]ou're going to do whatever I want you to do and then you can go; You'll be fine if you do it." There was also evidence that Veikoso used "[p]hysical force" to overcome CW # 2. CW # 2 testified that Veikoso struck her in the face and the back of the head several times, grabbed her hair, and pulled her down to the center console, causing her to bleed and "black[ ] out." She stated that when she attempted to free her hair from Veikoso's hands, he hit her on the back of the head with his fist or elbow. Once at the school, Veikoso dragged her by the hair to a bench before demanding her to perform oral and vaginal sex. He then placed his hands on her neck and pressed down on her throat, making it difficult for her to breathe, and ejaculated in her mouth.

CW # 2 testified that Veikoso continued to use force against her even after she started bleeding and blacked out. After being threatened and hit several times, CW # 2 began screaming, but Veikoso continued to threaten and use force against CW # 2. In addition, Veikoso threatened and used force against CW # 2 more than once. It may be inferred from the circumstances that Veikoso was "aware" he was using threats and force to overcome CW # 2, and therefore, knowingly subjected CW # 2 to acts of sexual penetration by strong compulsion.

In light of the foregoing, there was "overwhelming . . . evidence tending to show Veikoso guilty of Counts 4 and 5 beyond a reasonable doubt."

ANALYSIS

To establish the offense of sexual assault in the first degree, the prosecution must prove beyond a reasonable doubt that the defendant subjected his or her victim to an act of sexual penetration by "strong compulsion."

In this case, the defendant's dire threats and his repeated use of force on his victim clearly satisfied that element, and his convictions of rape were affirmed. Do note that Veikoso was charged with two counts of rape; that is, two separate charges. One count was based upon his act of forcing the victim to have oral sex with him, and the other count relates to his act of vaginal sex on his victim. The Hawaii Supreme Court found the elements of both of those offenses fully satisfied and affirmed his convictions on both counts. (Veikoso was sentenced to concurrent terms of 20 years in prison for these two convictions.)

CHAPTER 7

Criminal Defenses: Three Distinct Types

There are three distinct types of criminal defenses: (1) Failure-of-proof defenses, (2) affirmative defenses, and (3) nullification defenses.

A. FAILURE-OF-PROOF DEFENSES

As discussed in Chapter 6, criminal trials in this country consist of the prosecution's effort to establish every element of each charged crime beyond a reasonable doubt. Defense counsel, in turn, often defends his or her client by trying to "negative" one or more of the elements of each of those charged offenses by creating a reasonable doubt in the minds of the jurors.

By far and away the most common kind of defense in criminal cases is the "failure-of-proof" defense, i.e., defense counsel defends his or her client by establishing that the prosecution has not carried its burden of proving one or more elements of the crime beyond a reasonable doubt.

CASE 9. Cocaine in the car: The defense succeeds by negativing an element of the charged offense; in this case, the element of constructive possession. Here is an example of a decision that demonstrates just how the failure-of-proof defense works. Johnson wasn't guilty of possession of cocaine, the Mississippi Supreme Court concluded, because there was a reasonable doubt about whether he constructively possessed it.

But do note that defense counsel didn't manage to persuade the jury of

THE CAR WITH COCAINE

this point. Rather, the Supreme Court, looking at the facts adduced at trial after the fact, concluded that the prosecution had not proved constructive possession at trial beyond a reasonable doubt. *See* Chapter 11 for a discussion of the role of appellate courts in this regard.

ARVIN PHILLIP JOHNSON v. STATE OF MISSISSIPPI
81 So.3d 1020 (Miss. 2011).

The Court: On December 5, 2006, at approximately 6:25 p.m., agents from the Mississippi Bureau of Narcotics were in Marion County, Mississippi, conducting a drug buy/bust operation. The target of the operation was "Teddy," who allegedly was selling drugs out of a small, locally owned convenience store located on Highway 13 South. The narcotics agents used a wired, confidential informant to make contact with Teddy to buy some marijuana using marked "buy" money. When the informant arrived at the store to purchase drugs from Teddy, Teddy called a man named Walter to bring the marijuana to the store. Walter arrived with the drugs shortly thereafter, and Teddy sold the drugs to the informant. When the agents went to the store to arrest Teddy, they saw a car parked under the store's awning between the gas pumps and the front door of the convenience store. The car had not been at the station when Teddy had sold the drugs to the informant just a few minutes prior. The agents also saw an unknown individual, later identified as Alvin Phillip Johnson, near the car, talking to Teddy. To secure the scene, the agents handcuffed Johnson and Teddy and had them lie face down on the ground. After conducting a search of the nearby vehicle, the agents discovered a white, rock-like substance, later confirmed to be .7 gram of cocaine, above the car's driver-side visor. Johnson was convicted of possession of this cocaine and sentenced to sixteen years in the custody of the Mississippi Department of Corrections.

"[P]ossession of a controlled substance may be actual or constructive . . . ." Because Johnson did not have actual possession of the cocaine, Johnson was found guilty of constructive possession; he asserts that the State failed to prove both elements for constructive possession. "Proximity is usually an essential element, but by itself is not adequate in the absence of other incriminating circumstances." "Constructive possession may be shown by establishing that the drug involved was subject to [the defendant's] dominion or control." This Court has held that "absent some competent evidence connecting him with the contraband," the defendant is entitled to acquittal.

It is undisputed that the car in which the cocaine was found was not at the gas station at the time the informant bought the marijuana from Teddy. Neither was Johnson at the gas station at the time of the drug exchange. Both the vehicle and Johnson arrived at the gas station within the short time between the drug exchange and the MBN agents' arrival. However, the State presented no evidence showing that Johnson had driven the car to the gas station or that he had been a passenger of the car. The State failed to present sufficient evidence as to the ownership of the car or who actually removed the car after Teddy's arrest.

In addition to proving Johnson had dominion and control over the car, the State also is required to show additional incriminating circumstances. Specifically, the State must prove that Johnson was intentionally and consciously in possession of the cocaine. Johnson was not the owner of the car. Even if Johnson had been driving the car, the white plastic bag that contained the cocaine was above the sun visor, which was in the upright position. The agents did not find Johnson's fingerprints on the bag containing the cocaine. Agent Harless admitted he was not sure whether Johnson had ever handled the bag. Also, it was never determined whether Johnson had been in the car at any time. Therefore, the State presented no incriminating circumstances to support the inference that Johnson constructively possessed the cocaine found in the nearby vehicle.

The State has the burden to prove that Johnson was aware of the cocaine and intentionally possessed it. "[V]iewing the evidence in the light most favorable to the prosecution" as required by our standard of review, we do not agree that a rational trier of fact could find that the elements of constructive possession existed based on this evidence alone. Therefore, we reverse Johnson's conviction and render a judgment of acquittal.

ANALYSIS

Johnson's conviction for possession of cocaine was reversed because the prosecution did not meet its burden of proof beyond a reasonable doubt with respect to two elements of constructive possession—proximity and incriminating circumstances.

Defense counsel was successful, albeit only on appeal, in convincing the Mississippi Supreme Court that the prosecution had not carried its burden of proving one or more elements of the crime beyond a reasonable doubt. This is a failure-of-proof defense.

CASE 10. The shady contractor: The defense succeeds by negativing an element of the charged offense; in this case, the requisite criminal intent. Here is another example of the failure-of-proof defense. Pena, a contractor who accepted a $10,000 payment and then did not do the job he contracted to do, wasn't guilty of theft, the Texas Court of Appeals ruled, because there was a reasonable doubt about whether he possessed the relevant intent to deprive the owner of his money at the time he took possession of it.

You should also note that even though Pena escaped criminal culpability for his wrongdoing, the court of appeals makes clear that he may still possess civil liability for his actions. As previously discussed, the Criminal Law and the civil law simply do not apply in the same way, even where the facts involved are absolutely identical. *See* discussion in Chapter 1.

JOSE DE LEON PENA v. STATE OF TEXAS
2011 WL 3845761 (Tex. Ct. App.-Corpus Christi 2011).

The Court: After a jury trial, Jose De Leon Pena was convicted of the offense of theft of property valued between $1,500 and $20,000, a state-jail felony, and sentenced to 180 days of confinement in the State Jail Division of the Texas Department of Criminal Justice.

After firing their first contractor, Noe Perez and his wife Maria Perez, approached Pena regarding the construction of a new law office in the City of Edinburg. Pena had owned his construction business, "J. Pena Construction," for approximately 18 years, and had built hundreds of homes and numerous commercial structures. On May 14, 2008, the Perezes entered into a written construction agreement with Pena. The contract provided that Pena's company would be paid a lump sum total of $250,600 for the commercial construction project, and that a $2,000 non-refundable deposit, would be paid upon execution of the agreement. On May 27, 2008, the Perezes gave Pena the $2,000 non-refundable retainer fee.

On June 9, 2008, the Perezes delivered a $10,000 check, payable to J. Pena Construction, and which included the word "Building" for the description. Pena testified the Perezes gave him the check for him to commence construction, despite the fact their construction loan had not yet been approved. Both Noe and Maria Perez concurred that those funds were given as an advance. Pena thereafter hired workers, marked elevation and property lines, measured and marked the location where the building was to be constructed, laid ground work by clearing

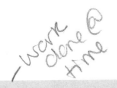

three to four inches of topsoil, hauled topsoil off the property, and brought in new dirt which was compacted with a backhoe and tractor.

Noe Perez applied for a $246,500 bank loan from the Bank of South Texas. On July 17, 2008, his application was presented to the loan committee. On August 18, 2008, the loan was approved, but Pena was not approved as the builder. Noe Perez's options were to either apply for a loan with another bank or use another builder, who could be approved by the bank. He decided to use another builder, notwithstanding the fact Pena had a signed contract with the Perezes and Pena had already commenced work under the contract. The contract did not address this contingency and did not provide that the Perezes could in effect fire Pena if the bank did not approve his company as the builder. Pena wanted to continue his work under the contract and Pena's bank was willing to provide Noe Perez a loan at a half percentage point lower interest. Noe Perez, however, was not interested.

On December 9, 2008, Noe Perez filed a police report, accusing Pena of theft of $10,000 and claiming Pena never performed any work. Pena was arrested on the felony charge of theft.

A claim of theft made in connection with a contract requires proof of more than an intent to deprive the owner of property and subsequent appropriation of the property. If no more than intent and appropriation is shown in a contract claim, nothing illegal is apparent, because under the terms of a contract, the individuals typically have the right to "deprive the owner of property," albeit in return for consideration. In a contract claim, the State must prove the defendant did not perform the contract and knew he was not entitled to the money, not merely that there is a dispute about the amount rightfully owed. The mere fact that one fails to return funds paid in advance after failing to perform a contract does not constitute theft. If money was voluntarily given to the defendant pursuant to a contractual agreement and there is insufficient evidence in the record to show the money was obtained by deception, the conviction cannot stand. For purposes of a theft conviction, the relevant intent to deprive the owner of his property is the accused's intent at the time of taking possession of the property.

The evidence presented shows only a civil contract dispute, and not the necessary criminal intent to support Pena's conviction. There is no evidence in the record that Pena did not fully intend to perform under the contract when he accepted the $10,000, and the evidence showed it was Noe Perez's decision to choose another builder while Pena wanted to continue working under the contract. Under every version of the facts presented by the trial witnesses, Pena performed at least some of the contractual work for the $10,000. We conclude the evidence is legally insufficient to sustain Pena's conviction because there is no evidence in the record of criminal intent to commit theft. We therefore reverse the judgment of conviction, dismiss the indictment, and render a judgment of acquittal.

ANALYSIS

Pena's conviction for theft of property was reversed because the prosecution did not meet its burden of proof beyond a reasonable doubt with respect to one of the elements of that offense: The intent to deprive the owner of his property at the time of taking possession of the property.

Defense counsel was successful, albeit only on appeal, in convincing the Texas Court of Appeals that the prosecution had not carried its burden of proving one of the elements of the crime beyond a reasonable doubt. This is a failure-of-proof defense.

B. AFFIRMATIVE DEFENSES

In addition to failure-of-proof defenses, criminal defense counsel often defend their clients by using so-called "affirmative defenses." With a failure-of-proof defense, as previously discussed, counsel is attempting to "negative" one or more of the elements of a charged offense by creating a reasonable doubt in the minds of the jurors. Affirmative defenses, in contrast, have nothing to do with the elements of the charged crime; an affirmative defense provides a defense without the necessity of having to negative an element of the crime.

An affirmative defense is a defense where *the defendant*—not the prosecution—has the burden of introducing evidence proving (usually by a preponderance of the evidence) each of the elements of an established (usually) statutory defense.

If the defense is successful, the defendant is acquitted—or, sometimes, depending on the statute, his or her offense is instead "mitigated" to a lower offense—despite the fact that all of the elements of the charged offense may have been established. In essence, the defendant is acquitted because his or her proof of the affirmative defense is viewed as justifying his otherwise criminal conduct.

Common examples of affirmative defenses recognized in all or most jurisdictions are duress, entrapment, insanity, necessity, self-defense, defense of others, defense of property, and defense of habitation.

The evidence offered by the defense in support of an affirmative defense can be either testimonial or physical. In fact, it can even be evidence that is obtained simply through cross examination of prosecution witnesses.

CASE 11. Mess with my antique car and I'll stab you: An affirmative defense is not made out unless the defense proves all of the elements of that defense; in this case, self-defense. Unlike a failure-of-proof defense where the defense need only create a reasonable doubt as to any element of the crime in order to be successful, the burden of proof with an affirmative defense, like self-defense in this case, is on the defendant. He or she needs to establish each and every one of the elements of that defense by a preponderance of the evidence, a significantly lower burden of proof than that placed on the prosecutor who must prove every element of a crime *beyond a reasonable doubt.*

In this case, the Louisiana Court of Appeals concluded that the defendant, Richard Jasper, did not successfully carry that burden on the question of who was the aggressor. The jury's conclusion that Jasper was the aggressor and that he did not prove to the jury's satisfaction that he stabbed his victim in self-defense was deemed to be entirely reasonable. Accordingly, his conviction was affirmed.

STATE OF LOUISIANA v. RICHARD D. JASPER
75 So.3d 984 (La. Ct. App. 3 Cir. 2011).

The Court: A jury found Richard Jasper guilty of aggravated battery and he was sentenced to twenty years at hard labor. Jasper appeals, asserting that the evidence presented at trial was insufficient to support his conviction. For the following reasons, we affirm.

Louisiana Revised Statutes 14:34 defines aggravated battery as "a battery committed with a dangerous weapon." Battery includes "the intentional use of force or violence upon the person of another."

Jasper contended that he acted in self-defense. However, an aggressor cannot claim self-defense, "unless he withdraws from the conflict in good faith and in such a manner that his adversary knows or should know that he desires to withdraw and discontinue the conflict."

It is the defendant's burden in a non-homicide to establish by a preponderance of the evidence that self-defense was justified. The State and Jasper offered two substantially different versions of the events leading to the stabbing of Mr. Louviere.

The State contended that, on January 8, 2008, after Jasper found that the windows on his antique car had been broken, he drove in a rage to Mr. Louviere's house, burst in uninvited and, after fighting with Mr. Louviere and his fiancée, Roxanna Garza, cut and/or stabbed Mr. Louviere in the face, neck and chest. In contrast to the State's version of the crime, Jasper contended that, after he found that the windows on his car had been broken out, he went to Mr. Louviere's home to confront him because, if Mr. Louviere had not caused the damage himself, he knew who did. Jasper claimed that although he yelled at Mr. Louviere, he was not physically aggressive until Mr. Louviere put the barrel of a rifle up to his head and cocked it. Jasper contended that his actions thereafter, including cutting Mr. Louviere, were in self-defense.

Our review of the record reveals that the evidence, viewed in the light most favorable to the prosecution, is sufficient to establish the elements of aggravated battery, i.e., that Jasper intentionally cut Mr. Louviere with a knife. We note that Jasper claimed that he acted in self-defense, however, it was his burden to prove this affirmative defense.

Although Jasper contends that the testimony given by State's witnesses was "incredible," credibility determinations are the province of the jury, which could have accepted the State's witnesses' version of the crime. Further, it was within the jury's purview to find that Jasper was the aggressor in the altercation and that he did not withdraw and, thus, reject his contention that he acted in self-defense.

ANALYSIS

Jasper's conviction for aggravated battery was upheld because he failed to meet his burden of convincing the jury that the affirmative defense of self-defense applied. The jurors considered his evidence and the prosecution's evidence, and they chose to believe the prosecution's account of what occurred, namely that Jasper was the aggressor in this situation and therefore was not entitled to acquittal on the basis of self-defense.

CASE 12. Beating for failure to pay drug money: An affirmative defense is not made out unless the defense proves all of the elements of that defense; in this case, duress. Just like Case 11, this decision demonstrates once again that the burden of proof with an affirmative defense, duress in this case, is on the defendant and that he or she must establish each and every one of the elements of that defense by a preponderance of the evidence. Defendant Dow's argument that the prosecution had the burden of proof was, the Washington Court of Appeals concluded, just plain wrong.

THE BURGLARY OF THE HOUSE TRAILER

The jury didn't believe Dow's duress claim, and the jurors' conclusion was a reasonable one. Hence, Dow's conviction was affirmed.

STATE OF WASHINGTON v. JEFFREY ALLEN DOW
162 Wash. App. 324, 253 P.3d 476 (Wash. Ct. App. Div. 2 2011).

The Court: A jury found Jeffrey Dow guilty of first degree burglary. Dow appeals, assigning error to the trial court's duress jury instruction. He asserts that the trial court did not explain that duress negates the intent element of burglary and requires that the State prove the absence of duress beyond a reasonable doubt.

Randy Blair testified that on the night of October 14, 2008, he woke up and found Paul Peterson and Dow inside his trailer home. Blair had previously purchased drugs from Peterson but had never met Dow. Peterson had a gun and demanded money from Blair to pay off a drug debt. When Blair said he did not have the money, Peterson looked at Dow and said, "[Y]ou know what you got to do." Dow then beat Blair's head and chest while Peterson pointed the gun in their direction. At some point during the beating, Blair noticed that Peterson had left the trailer with the gun and he began fighting back; Blair testified that he thought Dow did not know Peterson had left because Peterson had been standing behind Dow. Blair grabbed a propane bottle, began swinging it around to fend off Dow, and the two continued fighting for about three to five minutes. Eventually, Dow fled from the trailer, Blair followed him, and Blair saw Dow jump into Peterson's car and drive away. As a result of the attack, Blair sustained severe bruising on his head, a bloody nose, and two broken ribs.

At trial, Dow testified that on the night of the incident, he and Peterson ingested drugs together and then Peterson wanted to collect a drug debt from Dow. Peterson offered to forgive Dow's debt if he helped collect Blair's drug debt. Dow testified that there was no discussion of how they were going to collect the debt or that they would use violence to collect it, but Dow saw Peterson had a gun. Dow also testified that he was aware that Peterson's prior drug debt collection activities always involved getting "physical with somebody." Dow testified that he agreed to accompany Peterson because he was afraid of what Peterson might do to him if he refused. Dow testified that he believed if he did not cooperate with Peterson that he would be killed or seriously injured.

Dow asserts that the trial court erred by instructing the jury that he had the burden of proving by a preponderance of the evidence that he acted under duress. Dow argues that after he asserted his duress defense, the State had the burden to disprove duress beyond a reasonable doubt because duress negates the intent element of first degree burglary.

In order to prove first degree burglary, the State had to show that Dow (1) entered or remained unlawfully in a dwelling, (2) with an intent to commit a crime against a person or property therein, and (3) assaulted someone. Duress is an affirmative defense that must be established by a preponderance of the evidence. The burden of proving duress is on the defendant. Generally, the affirmative defense of duress does not negate an element of a charged offense; instead, a finding of duress excuses the defendant's otherwise unlawful conduct.

Here, the trial court properly instructed the jury on the law of duress and stated that "[t]he burden is on the defendant to prove the defense of duress by a preponderance of the evidence." The trial court's jury instruction allocating the burden of proving duress to Dow was not error.

ANALYSIS

Dow's conviction for first-degree burglary was upheld because he failed to meet his burden of convincing the jury by a preponderance of the evidence that the affirmative defense of duress applied. The jurors considered his evidence and the prosecution's evidence about his alleged intent, and they simply chose to believe the prosecution's account of what occurred; therefore, there was no error in the trial judge's instruction.

As you can tell from the foregoing discussion and the *Jasper* and *Dow* decisions set out in this chapter, it is more advantageous to a criminal defendant to make a failure-of-proof defense than an affirmative defense because the burden of proof is on the prosecution in the former case (beyond a reasonable doubt) and on the defendant in the latter (preponderance of the evidence). But all defense counsel can do is do the best that he or she can with the facts and circumstances with which he or she is presented. Sometimes, the best defense is a failure-of-proof defense; sometimes, it's an affirmative defense; sometimes, it's both.

And sometimes, neither of those types of defense is tenable.

C. CRIMINAL DEFENSE ETHICS

Sometimes, there simply is no viable defense. You probably won't be shocked to learn this, but sometimes, actually, a lot of the time, criminal defense counsel's client is just plain guilty . . . and there is no good failure-of-proof or affirmative defense to the charges brought against that accused person. *So what happens then?*

Here's the important point to bear in mind: The client—the accused—decides what happens then. Not defense counsel.

Lawyers—criminal defense counsel—are not judges or juries. They do not *adjudicate* their client's cases, they *defend* them. And the goals of that defense—unlike the manner in which the defense is undertaken—are up to the accused, the client. Put another way, as a matter of legal ethics, clients have the right—*the autonomy*—to make their own decisions about the aims of their representation. And this is true even if those aims or their decisions are ill-advised, unwise, or imprudent.

What does this actually mean *specifically*, in this setting?

Well, for one thing, it means that a guilty client may well decide that he or she wants to plead not guilty and to be defended as if he or she is not guilty. This happens commonly. Although defense counsel may advise against this position and may want to engage in plea negotiations with the prosecutor or to accept a proffered plea deal, the decision of whether or not to plead or negotiate is the criminal defendant's decision to make, not defense counsel's decision.

Defense counsel can *and should* give the client the benefit of his or her expertise, wisdom, and tactical and strategic insights. But, that said, ultimately what is on the line is *the defendant's* life, it's *the defendant's* freedom, it's *the defendant's* resources, and it's *the defendant*—not defense counsel—who has the right to make the ultimate decision whether to plead guilty or not guilty or whether or not to seek or accept a plea bargain.

Every U.S. jurisdiction, every state and federal judicial district, has a legal ethics code that applies to the lawyers practicing law in that Bar. The American Bar Association (ABA) has promulgated Model Rules of Professional Conduct (Model Rules), legal ethics rules, large portions of which have been adopted as the prevailing legal ethics rules in most states.

Pertaining to this discussion, ABA Model Rule 1.2(a) provides in relevant part, that "a lawyer shall abide by a client's decisions concerning the objectives of representation and . . . shall consult with the client as to the means by which they are to be pursued . . . *In a criminal case, the lawyer shall abide by the client's decision, after consultation with the lawyer, as to a plea to be entered*, whether to waive jury trial and whether the client will testify" (Emphasis added).

Similarly, the accused generally has the right, after consultation with defense counsel, to make a number of additional decisions for himself or herself, including what pleas to enter, whether to accept a plea agreement, whether to waive jury trial, whether to testify in his or her own defense, and whether to appeal.

There's an important caveat here. The accused has the right to make the decision of whether or not to plead guilty or not guilty. That does not mean, however, that when a defendant actually decides to plead not guilty and to go to trial, he or she also has the right to dictate exactly how the defense must proceed. Defense counsel must accede to his or her client's decision about the plea, as discussed, but in defending that client at trial, defense counsel still has the strict and overriding obligation to follow the law and the prevailing ethical rules.

Defense counsel has the right, however, to determine *the manner* in which the defense is actually undertaken. In essence, defense counsel makes the tactical and strategic decisions, although consultation with the client is appropriate when it is feasible. These decisions include what witnesses to call and what to ask them, whether and how to conduct cross examination of the prosecution's witnesses, what jurors to accept or strike, what motions to make at trial, and what evidence should or should not be introduced.

The issue remains—what happens if a loyal, diligent, competent defense attorney reviews and investigates everything involved in the case and nonetheless determines that there is no tenable legal defense to be made to the charges brought against his or her client? *What then?*

Well, as noted before, that attorney should tell the client precisely that. The lawyer should also make whatever appropriate suggestions to the client that might reasonably follow from that conclusion, e.g., "You should let me try to negotiate a favorable plea agreement for you." But what if the client *still* insists on going to trial? Once again, *that* is the client's right—ethically and constitutionally. What defense counsel should do in that situation is to go to trial and in the phrase that is often used in this setting, "put the State to its proofs."

As ABA Model Rule 3.1 provides, making this point in a similar fashion: "[a] lawyer shall not bring or defend a proceeding, or assert or controvert an issue therein, unless there is a basis in law and fact for doing so that is not frivolous, which includes a good faith argument for an extension, modification or reversal of existing law. *A lawyer for the defendant in a criminal proceeding, or the respondent in a proceeding that could result in incarceration, may nevertheless so defend the proceeding as to require that every element of the case be established.*" (Emphasis added.)

At the very minimum, "defend the proceeding as to require that every element of the case be established." That's defense counsel's obligation, when and if that reflects the client's wishes, even where defense counsel does not believe that he or she has any other viable means of effective defense.

Pay close attention to the description of criminal defense counsel's actions at trial that you will see described in some of the appellate cases that you will be reading in your Criminal Law class. When you do, you'll see many examples of defense counsel defending his or her client simply by putting the State to its proofs. The preceding discussion should help you see why that is the case.

D. NULLIFICATION DEFENSE

As mentioned at the beginning of this chapter, there is a third type of defense that defense counsel often make in criminal trials—a nullification defense.

Now, strictly speaking, a nullification defense is not really a formal, legal defense at all. Rather, it is an attempt by defense counsel to sway the jurors to one degree or another by presenting a narrative, a "story," to them that might, hopefully, from defense counsel's point of view, cause them to sympathize with the accused and "nullify" the law.

Recall the general discussion in Chapter 5 of jury nullification:

> "One of the implications of the possibility of jury nullification in our criminal justice system is that lawyers, criminal defense counsel, *and* prosecutors will often attempt to influence jurors to focus on something other than the elements of criminal offenses and defenses that they are instructed to focus upon by the trial judge

because they know that juries can ignore the law. The lawyers can't do this openly and expressly because even though juries can ignore the law, they can't be encouraged to do it. But that doesn't mean jury nullification won't happen. It does.

A criminal defense attorney might, for example, try to get the jury to consider and sympathize with his or her client's terrible, abusive upbringing, the extenuating circumstances the accused was facing, the failings of the alleged victim, or the brutality of the police in arresting him. A prosecutor, in contrast, might want the jurors to consider and sympathize with the victim's suffering or that of the victim's family, the antisocial personality of the accused, or the criminal nature of his or her associates or associations."

In short, coupled with the more formal failure-of-proof and affirmative defenses, defense counsel sometimes try to defend their clients by presenting to the jury a story (or stories) that they think might cause the jurors to ignore the law to the benefit of their clients. Such defensive tactics are not always lawful . . . or ethical.

As discussed previously in Chapter 5 and in the excerpt from that chapter set out here, defense counsel are not permitted to make empathetic arguments like this openly. But that doesn't mean that it does not happen anyway. Defense counsel sometimes engages in such tactical behavior in a number of different ways.

For example, counsel may try and make a point to the jury by implication through a question to a witness: "Did you realize that my client was sexually abused as a child by both of her parents?" Whatever answer the witness gives in response, defense counsel has made the point he or she wanted to make; i.e., my client was abused as a child.

This sort of inferential communication also takes place on occasion during the jury selection process via questions asked to the venire (potential jurors), such as "Would you hold the fact that my client was sexually abused as a child by both of her parents against her during these trial proceedings?" See? Point made.

Now, bear in mind that the presentation of such an inferential—jury nullification—focused—argument is, or at least should be, subject to the normal rules of evidence and legal ethics.

As an evidentiary matter, much of the story of the sort that criminal defense counsel might want to "tell" ("My client is a victim of law enforcement racism," for example) would be irrelevant, at least as a legal matter. Hence, in the absence of a good (if ingenuous) reason supporting its admission as relevant to some legal point, such "story-telling" would be inadmissible, assuming that the prosecutor is on the ball and objects to its admission and the trial judge agrees.

Moreover, as a matter of legal ethics, criminal defense counsel needs to follow the rules of evidence closely. Counsel should not, for example, try to bring inadmissible matter up in court or make impermissible comments or arguments. And defense counsel is acting unethically when and if he or she makes comments on or off the record in a manner that is calculated to influence a jury.

Improper as these comments and actions may be, they happen. Read news accounts of current criminal trials. Watch the comments of criminal defense counsel on television. The fact that nullification defenses are used is not a secret. It's a fact of life in our criminal justice system.

What do you think? Is it appropriate? Should we—can we—do something to keep this sort of defense from occurring?

CASE 13. Crack rock in the swimming pool defense: Defense counsel will often try to persuade the jury to ignore the law. Since juries can ignore the law if they want to, defense counsel often try to send a message to the jurors encouraging them to do just that. That's what happened in this Texas case. Texas law now provides that the weight of a controlled substance for purposes of sentencing enhancement applies both to the weight of the narcotic substance itself *and* any additional substances with which it is mixed. (Narcotics are commonly combined with other substances in order to increase the amount that can be sold. This is often called "cutting.")

Despite that law, defendant Marchand's defense counsel tried to convey to the jury the notion that they should *only* consider the amount of "pure" cocaine in deciding which narcotics offense his client committed. As the federal district court concluded, that type of attempted nullification defense was perfectly reasonable.

By the way, the reason that this is a 2010 *federal* decision, although Marchand's criminal trial took place in a Texas *state* court in 1999, is that this proceeding was Marchand's present counsel's attempt to obtain a writ of habeas corpus for him in federal court, 11 years after his conviction. A writ of habeas corpus is a judicial order that a convicted person be freed because he or she was subjected to a violation of his or her constitutional rights by the State courts. As you will see, his petition for the writ of habeas corpus was denied.

DOUGLAS WILLFRED MARCHAND v. RICK THALER, DIRECTOR, TEXAS DEPARTMENT OF CRIMINAL JUSTICE, CORRECTIONAL INSTITUTIONS DIVISION
2010 WL 3239151 (N.D. Tex. 2010).

The Court: Douglas Willfred Marchand seeks to challenge on habeas corpus the validity of his 1999 Wilbarger County, Texas conviction.

Marchand was indicted by a Wilbarger County grand jury for the offense of possession of a controlled substance with an intent to manufacture that substance. Marchand was tried by jury, found guilty, and sentenced to ninety-five (95) years in prison.

Marchand's complaints concerning the ineffectiveness of his counsel arise out of the circumstance that for many years prior to the date of his indictment and trial, Texas courts had previously ruled that in order to sustain a conviction for one of the enhanced provisions of possession, delivery or manufacture of a controlled substance that depended upon the weight of the controlled substance possessed, the State had to prove the weight of the pure substance exclusive of any adulterants or dilutants or prove the weight of the adulterants or dilutants in the mixture to back into the weight of the pure substance.

In 1997, two years prior to Marchand's prosecution, the Texas Legislature added to the definition of "controlled substance" the sentence, "The term includes the aggregate weight of any mixture, solution, or other substance containing a controlled substance." Marchand contends that his trial counsel, Marty Cannedy, was unaware of this "change in the law" and had not adequately researched the law applicable to Marchand's case, had erroneously planned a deficient defense based upon the out-dated definition of controlled substances which lacked the qualifying sentence, ineffectively cross-examined the state's experts on the quantity or weight issue, and made an ineffective motion for directed verdict, all relying on his erroneous understanding of the law. Hence, claims Marchand, his trial counsel was ineffective.

At the hearing before the trial court after remand from the Court of Criminal Appeals, Cannedy testified that he was aware of the law change. But whether he was aware of or disagreed with the effect of the statutory change, it is clear that throughout the trial Cannedy highlighted the State's failure to prove the amount (quantity or weight) of the "pure" controlled substance as a condition to a conviction under the indictment. He argued the weight issue in support of his motion to dismiss the indictment, he argued the issue in making objections to the court's charge to the jury, in his oral motion for directed verdict, and in his argument to the jury. Thus Cannedy established a factual basis to argue to the jury that they should consider only the amount of "pure" methamphetamine in Marchand's possession, not the overall weight of the mixtures; in essence, a plea for jury nullification. This is recognized as the "Crack Rock in the Swimming Pool" argument, an analogy that asks the jury in a drug manufacturing case to consider (at either the guilt-innocence or punishment stage) whether a rock (pebble-sized) of crack (cocaine) in a swimming pool converted the whole pool of swimming pool water into cocaine. This analogy is used to entice a jury into considering either finding guilt of a lesser included offense or making a not-guilty finding, or finding a lesser number of years' punishment, in order to punish the prosecution for "overreaching."

I find that all of Marchand's challenges to the effectiveness of counsel fail. I find that Marchand's trial counsel's conduct did not fall below the objective standard of reasonableness. I further find that Marchand has failed to demonstrate that his trial "counsel's errors were so egregious as to deprive the defendant of a fair trial whose result is reliable." I recommend that Marchand's claims for relief based upon the conduct of his trial counsel be denied.

ANALYSIS

The fact that Marchand's defense counsel attempted to make a "Crack Rock in the Swimming Pool" jury nullification defense did not render his representation constitutionally ineffective. The habeas corpus court found this approach to be a reasonable one, despite the fact that it failed.

Parenthetically, the reason you saw the court's use of the first-person "I" in the last paragraph of the court opinion above is that this particular opinion came from a single-judge federal district court. Most of the opinions you read in casebooks, in contrast, are the opinions of multi-judge appellate courts. As a result, even though a single judge or justice is writing the opinion, he or she is usually writing for himself or herself and for other judges or justices as well, and so the more common personal reference is "we," such as "We hold that the lower court decision is reversed."

CHAPTER 8

What Conduct Is Criminalized and Why?

A. COMMON LAW CRIMES AND "THE RECEPTION"

U.S. law, including our Criminal Law, has its roots in the English Common Law.

What does that mean exactly?

Well, U.S. attorneys use the phrase "common law" in two distinct ways. We may be distinguishing between the Anglo-American legal systems, which are focused upon case law interpretation of legislation, as opposed to European "civil law" systems, which focus upon application of statutory codes. Here, however, the term Common Law refers to the body of governing legal principles that was established by the courts of England prior to the colonial period. This Common Law was transplanted to the English colonies and subsequently became part of the law of the United States.

Even after the American Revolution took place and we gained our independence from England, the federal government and each of the states in the fledgling United States continued to use English Common Law as the governing law and precedent. The decision to use pre-Independence English Common Law as the starting point for U.S. law is called "the Reception." The English Common Law was "received" by the national government and by the states, as opposed to those jurisdictions trying to quickly craft a new set of applicable laws.

Of course, over time, the laws *did* change in the federal system and in the individual states. Many Common Law legal principles were abandoned, either by legislation or by judicial interpretation, or by both. And new statutes, thousands and eventually tens of thousands of new statutes, were enacted in every U.S. jurisdiction. Often this new legislation dealt with subject matter that would have been wholly unknown and foreign to the common law courts, e.g., the regulation of motorized vehicles.

An important part of the Common Law that was brought over to the colonies and ultimately to the new U.S. states was the Common Law crimes.

Over time in medieval England, the traditional recourse to violent "blood feuds" to remedy violent wrongdoing was replaced by a limited set of specifically defined Common Law crimes that were available to be prosecuted in the Common Law courts.

These Common Law crimes included the following offenses:

- Murder,
- manslaughter,
- mayhem,
- rape,
- larceny,
- robbery,
- burglary,
- arson,
- assault and battery,
- perjury,
- forgery, and
- bribery.

As a result of the Reception, each of these offenses—including the specific elements that comprised each of these offenses at Common Law—became a part of the Crimes Code of every U.S. jurisdiction at the time of the founding of this Nation.

Today, Common Law crimes have been expressly abrogated in most U.S. jurisdictions. *See,* for example, 18 Pa. Cons. Stat. §107(b) ("Common law crimes abolished—No conduct constitutes a crime unless it is a crime under this title or another statute of this Commonwealth") and N.J. Stat. §2C:1-5(a) ("Common law crimes are abolished and no conduct constitutes an offense unless the offense is defined by this code or another statute of this State").

But this hasn't happened everywhere. For example, in the Michigan Crimes Code, Mich. Comp. Laws §750.321 provides as follows: "Manslaughter—Any person who shall commit the crime of manslaughter shall be guilty of a felony punishable by imprisonment in the state prison, not more than 15 years or by fine of not more than 7,500 dollars, or both, at the discretion of the court." *But what are the elements of manslaughter?* The statute is silent. That is because the definition of the offense is still—even today—taken from the English Common Law. See, for example, *People v. Richardson*, 409 Mich. 126, 134 n.8, 293 N.W.2d 332, 335 n. 8 (1980) ("Our manslaughter statute does not define that offense, but instead incorporates the common-law definition").

Indeed, even in jurisdictions where the Common Law has been expressly abrogated for all crimes, courts continue to look to the Common Law origins of Criminal Law offenses to shed light on their modern interpretation.

CASE 14. Drunk driving homicide: English Common Law principles continue to be important in the interpretation of criminal statutes. In a setting where the Iowa legislature did not indicate that it wanted to make a change from the use of Common Law principles relating to the crime of vehicular homicide, the Iowa Supreme Court continues to apply them. This is a common approach taken by state courts. But do note that where the state legislature wants to make a change from the Common Law, it has every right and authority to do that.

STATE OF IOWA v. JONATHAN Q. ADAMS
810 N.W.2d 365 (Iowa 2012).

The Court: On the evening of December 8, 2006, Jonathan Adams attended a party at a friend's house in Des Moines. By his own admission, he consumed between three and five beers over a five-hour period and may have drunk twice that much. At about 10:45 p.m., he and an acquaintance, Sean Erickson, left the party in Adams' car with Adams driving. The right headlight on Adams' car was not functioning. As they traveled westbound on Park Avenue, Adams' car struck Tina Marie Brown, who was bicycling in the right hand lane, also heading west. Brown was propelled onto the hood of the car, and her head struck the windshield, shattering the passenger side. Brown died from her injuries. Adams was charged with murder by vehicle, operating while intoxicated, and leaving the scene of an accident, and was convicted on all three counts.

Iowa Code section 707.6A(1) provides: "A person commits a felony when the person unintentionally causes the death of another *by* operating a motor vehicle while intoxicated . . . ." (Emphasis added.) Adams contends the word "by" in section 707.6A(1) expresses a legislative intent that a conviction may be had under the statute only upon proof that the defendant's intoxication was the proximate cause of another's death. The State, however, asserts the plain language of subsection (1) demonstrates the legislature did not intend to require a causal connection between the defendant's intoxication and the victim's death.

Because we think there is more than one plausible interpretation of the statute, we must look beyond the plain language of the statute to resolve the ambiguity. Our goal is to ascertain and effectuate the true legislative intent. We examine the language of the statute, its underlying purpose and policies, and the consequences stemming from different interpretations. In doing so, we must construe the statute in its entirety. If more than one statute relating to the subject matter at issue is relevant to the inquiry, we consider all the statutes together in an effort to harmonize them.

In determining the intent of the legislature, we will not construe the language of a statute to produce an absurd or impractical result. We presume the legislature intends a reasonable result when it enacts a statute. Additionally, we strictly construe criminal statutes' and resolve doubts in favor of the accused.

Prior to the enactment of section 707.6A explicitly addressing homicide by vehicle, vehicular homicide cases were prosecuted under a manslaughter statute according to common law principles. We concluded the State must "show a direct causal connection between defendant's drunken driving and the death." Such was the state of the law when section 707.6A was enacted in 1986 and codified in 1987. In construing statutes, we assume the legislature is familiar with the existing state of the law when it enacts new legislation. Further, "[a] statute will not be presumed to overturn long-established legal principles, unless that intention is clearly expressed or the implication to that effect is inescapable."

The new statutory framework included no clear expression of the legislature's intent as to whether the State must prove a direct causal connection between the defendant's intoxicated driving and the victim's death to support a conviction. In such instances of ambiguity, we rely upon the rule of construction that presumes the legislature did not intend to overturn long-established legal principles in the absence of a clear expression of an intent to do so.

We conclude it is the State's burden under section 707.6A(1) to prove a causal connection between the defendant's intoxicated driving and the victim's death. Although the statute does not impose a burden on the State to prove a specific causal connection between the defendant's intoxication and the victim's death, it does require proof of a factual causal connection between a specific criminal act—"intoxicated driving"—and the victim's death. Put another way, the statute demands more than mere proof that the defendant's driving caused the death of another person. A defendant may be found guilty of homicide by vehicle only if the jury finds beyond a reasonable doubt that his criminal act of driving under the influence of alcohol caused the victim's death.

ANALYSIS

The Iowa Supreme Court found that the relevant portion of the murder by vehicle statute required the State to prove a causal connection between the defendant's intoxicated driving and the victim's death. Because such cases were previously prosecuted under a manslaughter statute "according to common law principles" and because the legislature gave no indication that its intent was to change that approach with this new statute, the same Common Law principles continue to apply.

Parenthetically but significantly for the defendant Adams, even though the court concluded that a causal tie between intoxicated driving and the victim's death must be proven, it nonetheless *affirmed* Adams' conviction for that crime because his trial counsel never raised that issue to the trial court and there may have been plausible strategic reasons why counsel chose not to raise that issue.

CASE 15. Wire theft from a mobile home: English Common Law principles continue to be important in the interpretation of criminal statutes. As in Case 14, the court interpreted significant statutory language, the word "curtilage" here, by reference to its meaning at Common Law. Using the Common Law definition of this term, the court concludes that the prosecution erred in its description of the term.

But that wasn't the end of the matter, as you will see. Because the Florida Court of Appeal found that this error wasn't "fundamental," it affirmed Dicks' conviction anyway.

This type of appellate analysis is common. *See* the related discussion in Chapter 11. Most often, this approach is called "harmless error analysis." No criminal trial is perfect. As a result, if any error that did occur did not affect the fundamental fairness of the proceeding, the verdict of guilty is affirmed *despite the error*. (In sports, by analogy, sometimes this type of approach is called the "no harm, no foul" rule.)

WILLIAM DICKS v. STATE OF FLORIDA
75 So.3d 857 (Fla. Ct. App. 1 Dist. 2011).

The Court: On the morning of April 1, 2010, Bohman Kirby was driving past rural land he owned in Columbia County when he noticed fresh tire tracks leading onto the property. Located on the property was a vacant mobile home that had been used as a residence by him and his family and, later, as rental property. On this particular morning, when he also observed the meter box had been pulled from its pole, Kirby stopped to investigate and saw that some cinder blocks used to surround a fire pit had been moved to allow a vehicle to back up to the mobile home. As he walked around the home, he also discovered that wires leading to the meter and the air conditioning unit had been cut and the back door had been pried open. Kirby looked inside a nearby utility shed and realized furniture he had been storing there was missing.

Kirby called the Columbia County Sheriff's Office. When Deputy Jonathan Rhodes arrived, he saw a bag of tools, a "Sawzall" and some copper wiring on the ground, none of which had been there that morning. In addition, he noticed an "egg crate" foam mattress lying on the ground—which Kirby later identified as having come from the utility shed—and discovered that the hole in the skirting appeared to have been enlarged. Using a flashlight, Deputy Rhodes looked into the hole and saw a man, later identified as Dicks, wearing work gloves and trying to hide behind the mobile home's cement support blocks. Dicks' brother was also under the home and wearing work gloves. Kirby later testified that so much wire had been removed, the mobile home was no longer capable of receiving power and all of the utilities required rewiring.

Dicks was charged by amended information with burglary of a dwelling by unlawfully entering a dwelling with the intent to commit theft. The term "dwelling" is defined by statute to mean "a building or conveyance of any kind, including any attached porch . . . , which has a roof over it and is designed to be occupied by people lodging therein at night, together with the curtilage thereof."

During closing arguments, the prosecutor "paraphrased" the statutory definition by describing a dwelling as "a building with a roof designed to be occupied by persons[,] together with the yard and the outbuildings immediately surrounding it." Moreover, when addressing whether Dicks had "entered" the dwelling, the prosecutor described the "backyard" as part of the dwelling, and argued that by Dicks' having "merely" entered the backyard of the mobile home, he had entered into the dwelling.

At the close of the arguments, the trial court read the following instruction concerning burglary of a dwelling: "Dwelling means a building of any kind, whether such a building is temporary or permanent, mobile or immobile, which has a roof over it and is designed to be occupied by people lodging therein at night, together with the enclosed space of ground and outbuildings immediately surrounding it. For purposes of burglary, a dwelling includes an attached porch or attached garage." At the conclusion of the trial, the jury returned a verdict of guilty as charged.

There is no dispute that the prosecutor's definition of a dwelling expressed an erroneous interpretation of the law. Although the statute defines both a structure and a dwelling to include "the curtilage thereof," it omits a definition of the term "curtilage." However, the Florida Supreme Court has ruled that the term "curtilage," as contemplated by the legislature in the burglary statute, "carr[ies] forward the common law requirement of some form of enclosure in order for the area surrounding a residence to be considered part of the 'curtilage' as referred to in the burglary statute."

Notwithstanding the prosecutor's error, Dicks concedes his failure to object precludes appellate review of this issue unless he can demonstrate the prosecutor's remarks constitute fundamental error. On this record, we conclude the prosecutor's comments did not rise to the level of fundamental error. That is because they did not reach down into the validity of the trial itself to the extent that a verdict of guilty could not have been obtained without the assistance of the alleged error. Accordingly, the judgment of conviction and sentence for burglary of a dwelling is hereby AFFIRMED.

ANALYSIS

The crime of burglary of a dwelling in Florida includes intrusion onto the "curtilage" of the property as that term was defined at Common Law where some type of enclosure was required. Hence, the prosecutor erred by arguing that mere entry into the backyard was sufficient to establish this element of the offense. Nonetheless, Dicks' conviction was affirmed because the prosecutor's error was not deemed to be fundamental.

B. POLITICS AND THE LEGISLATIVE PROCESS

After the American Revolution, Congress and all of the new state legislatures began enacting legislation, including many new criminal offenses, as well as significant amendments to existing Common Law crimes. In the Eighteenth Century, many of these newly enacted criminal offenses focused upon moral issues, criminalizing fornication, adultery, bestiality, and public drunkenness, for example. By the Nineteenth Century, many of the newly enacted criminal offenses adopted by Congress and the state legislatures sought to protect economic, rather than moral or ideological, interests.

The question often arises: What limits are there on the activities that can lawfully be criminalized by Congress . . . or by any state legislature? The quick answer to this question is an easy one: *There are virtually no limits!*

The point is that, for the most part, legislatures can simply criminalize whatever they want to criminalize!

"Wait," you interject (I'm speaking for you here), "but that means that the enactment of some criminal offenses will essentially reflect the wishes of special interest groups or transient moral outrage or political or ideological or religious agendas."

To which, I respond: "Exactly. You've got it."

The legislative process is a *political* process. And I'm trying to use the word "political" here in a nonpejorative fashion. Legislatures are *supposed to* be political. Legislators are supposed to listen to the desires and priorities and wishes of their constituents. That's why they were elected.

So when the people, in their wisdom, "throw the rascals out" and elect new representatives (*new rascals?*), *well* . . . you can expect that *new* laws, including new criminal offenses, will subsequently be enacted to reflect the new political agenda that the voters seemingly approved in electing new representatives.

That's what is supposed to happen. It's politics, yes. It's politics. But it's also what legislatures and legislative representatives are *supposed* to do: Reflect the will of the people.

C. CONSTITUTIONAL LIMITATIONS ON CRIMINALIZATION

Now, despite everything I just told you in the preceding section, there are *some* limits on what can be criminalized. I know I just said that *"there are virtually no limits."* But . . . the fledgling lawyers among you will have already seized upon the use of the word "virtually" in that sentence. There are *some* limits . . . they simply don't apply to very much criminal legislation. For the most part, legislatures can simply criminalize whatever they want to criminalize.

What are those minimal limits on what can be criminalized? They reflect the application of constitutional law and they include limitations like the following:

- **Privacy Protections.** The Supreme Court has made clear that individuals are entitled to certain privacy rights under the U.S. Constitution that cannot be compromised by criminal legislation. Certainly the best known of these rights is a woman's right to choose whether she wants to have an abortion prior to the viability of her fetus. State legislatures cannot criminalize that decision previability. Nor, since 2003, as another example, can state legislatures criminalize homosexual activity taking place between consenting adults.
- **Equal Protection Problems.** Legislatures cannot enact criminal statutes that impermissibly discriminate between certain groups of people, e.g., making something a crime only for members of one race or gender.
- **Cruel and Unusual Punishment Issues.** There are some constitutional limitations on what punishment can be prescribed for certain criminal activity. For example, the Supreme Court has held that the death penalty may not be lawfully imposed upon juveniles and what the Court refers to as "mentally retarded" persons or someone who has raped but not killed an adult woman.
- **Free Speech Limits.** Legislatures cannot criminalize actions that involve protected (First Amendment) speech. For example, the Supreme Court has held that states cannot criminalize an individual's expressive act of burning an American flag as a form of protest.
- **Due Process Problems.** A criminal statue may be unconstitutional as "void for vagueness," thus violating the due process clause of the Fourteenth Amendment to the U.S. Constitution. A statute is unconstitutionally vague if it fails to define the criminal offense with sufficient definiteness that ordinary people can understand what conduct is prohibited or if it contains definitions that encourages arbitrary and discriminatory enforcement.

This is not an exhaustive list of constitutional limitations on criminal legislation, but it accounts for a good deal, if not most, of the restrictions on a legislature's ability to criminalize particular conduct. Please remember that these limitations do *not* apply, however, to the great majority of statutory enactments. For the most part, legislatures can do whatever they want.

CASE 16. Depictions of animal cruelty: There are some constitutional limitations on what a legislature can criminalize. For the most part, legislatures can do whatever they want. But, as this United States Supreme Court decision illustrates, they can't criminalize everything.

Robert Stevens ran a business called Dogs of Velvet and Steel, through which he sold videos of pit bulls engaging in dogfights and attacking other animals. Among these videos were "Japan Pit Fights" and "Pick-A-Winna: A Pit Bull Documentary," which included footage of dogfights in Japan (where such conduct is allegedly legal) as well as footage of American dogfights from the 1960s and 1970s. A third video, "Catch Dogs and Country Living," depicted the use of pit bulls to hunt wild boar, as well as a gruesome scene of a pit bull attacking a domestic farm pig. On the basis of these videos, Stevens was indicted and convicted of three counts of violating a federal statute criminalizing depictions of animal cruelty. However, as you will see, the Supreme Court ruled—applying First Amendment free speech protections—that Congress did not have the power to criminalize conduct like this.

But keep reading to the end of the decision. As the Supreme Court often does, it confined its decision to the narrow confines of the case that was before it—in this case, a very broadly inclusive statute. Lawyers who follow the court would pay close attention to the last paragraph below where the Court says, "[w]e need not and do not decide whether a statute limited to crush videos or other depictions of extreme animal cruelty would be constitutional." Note that the question of the lawfulness of a more narrowly drafted criminal statute is left for another day.

UNITED STATES v. ROBERT J. STEVENS,
130 S. Ct. 1577, 176 L. Ed.2d 435 (2010).

The Court: Congress enacted 18 U.S.C. §48 to criminalize the commercial creation, sale, or possession of certain depictions of animal cruelty. The statute does not address underlying acts harmful to animals, but only portrayals of such conduct. The question presented is whether the prohibition in the statute is consistent with the freedom of speech guaranteed by the First Amendment.

The Government's primary submission is that §48 necessarily complies with the Constitution because the banned depictions of animal cruelty, as a class, are categorically unprotected by the First Amendment. We disagree. The First Amendment provides that "Congress shall make no law . . . abridging the freedom of speech." As a general matter, the First Amendment means that government has no power to restrict expression because of its message, its ideas, its subject matter, or its content. Section 48 explicitly regulates expression based on content: The statute restricts "visual [and] auditory depiction[s]," such as photographs, videos, or sound recordings, depending on whether they depict conduct in which a living animal is intentionally harmed. As such, §48 is presumptively invalid, and the Government bears the burden to rebut that presumption.

From 1791 to the present, however, the First Amendment has permitted restrictions upon the content of speech in a few limited areas,

and has never included a freedom to disregard these traditional limitations. These historic and traditional categories long familiar to the bar,
including obscenity, defamation, fraud, incitement, and speech integral
to criminal conduct, are well-defined and narrowly limited classes of
speech, the prevention and punishment of which have never been
thought to raise any Constitutional problem. The Government argues
that depictions of animal cruelty should be added to the list. It contends
that depictions of "illegal acts of animal cruelty" that are "made, sold, or
possessed for commercial gain" necessarily "lack expressive value," and
may accordingly "be regulated as unprotected speech." The claim is not
just that Congress may regulate depictions of animal cruelty subject to
the First Amendment, but that these depictions are outside the reach of
that Amendment altogether—that they fall into a "'First Amendment
Free Zone.'"

The First Amendment's guarantee of free speech does not extend
only to categories of speech that survive an ad hoc balancing of relative
social costs and benefits. The First Amendment itself reflects a judgment
by the American people that the benefits of its restrictions on the Government outweigh the costs. Our Constitution forecloses any attempt to
revise that judgment simply on the basis that some speech is not worth
it. The Constitution is not a document prescribing limits, and declaring
that those limits may be passed at pleasure.

Not to worry, the Government says: The Executive Branch construes
§48 to reach only "extreme" cruelty, and it "neither has brought nor will
bring a prosecution for anything less." The Government hits this theme
hard, invoking its prosecutorial discretion several times. But the First
Amendment protects against the Government; it does not leave us at
the mercy of noblesse oblige. We would not uphold an unconstitutional
statute merely because the Government promised to use it responsibly.

We need not and do not decide whether a statute limited to crush
videos or other depictions of extreme animal cruelty would be
constitutional. We hold only that §48 is not so limited but is instead substantially overbroad, and therefore invalid under the First Amendment.

ANALYSIS

The federal statute criminalizing the commercial creation, sale, or possession of certain depictions of animal cruelty was held to be unconstitutional as
void for vagueness. Applying First Amendment free speech principles, the
Court held that Congress could not criminalize this conduct based solely
upon the content of these depictions.

CASE 17. Juveniles sentenced to life without parole: There are some constitutional limitations on what a legislature can criminalize. Once again, as this Supreme Court decision illustrates, legislatures simply can't criminalize everything.

In the *Graham* decision set out below, due to the Eighth Amendment's prohibition on cruel and unusual punishments, the Supreme Court held that legislatures do not have the power to enact sentencing statutes that empower courts to sentence juvenile offenders to life without the possibility of parole *for nonhomicide offenses.*

Parenthetically, subsequent to *Graham*, the Supreme Court even more recently ruled that a *mandatory* life imprisonment without parole sentence for those under the age of 18 at the time of their crimes also violates the Eighth Amendment's prohibition on cruel and unusual punishments. *Miller v. Alabama*, 132 S. Ct. 2455, 183 L. Ed.2d 407 (2012).

TERRANCE JAMMAR GRAHAM v. STATE OF FLORIDA
130 S. Ct. 2011, 176 L. Ed.2d 825 (2010).

The Court: The issue before the Court is whether the Constitution permits a juvenile offender to be sentenced to life in prison without parole for a nonhomicide crime.

The Eighth Amendment states: "Excessive bail shall not be required, nor excessive fines imposed, nor cruel and unusual punishments inflicted." To determine whether a punishment is cruel and unusual, courts must look beyond historical conceptions to the evolving standards of decency that mark the progress of a maturing society. This is because the standard of extreme cruelty is not merely descriptive, but necessarily embodies a moral judgment. The standard itself remains the same, but its applicability must change as the basic mores of society change. The Cruel and Unusual Punishments Clause prohibits the imposition of inherently barbaric punishments under all circumstances. Punishments of torture, for example, are forbidden. These cases underscore the essential principle that, under the Eighth Amendment, the State must respect the human attributes even of those who have committed serious crimes.

The Court's cases addressing the proportionality of sentences fall within two general classifications. The first involves challenges to the length of term-of-years sentences given all the circumstances in a particular case. The second comprises cases in which the Court implements the proportionality standard by certain categorical restrictions on the death penalty. In the first classification the Court considers all of the circumstances of the case to determine whether the sentence is unconstitutionally excessive. The second classification of cases has used categorical rules to define Eighth Amendment standards. The previous cases in this classification involved the death penalty. The classification in turn consists of two subsets, one considering the nature of the offense, the other considering the characteristics of the offender. With respect to the nature of the offense, the Court has concluded that capital punishment is impermissible for nonhomicide crimes against individuals. In cases turning on the characteristics of the offender, the Court has adopted categorical rules prohibiting the death penalty for defendants who committed their crimes before the age of 18, or whose intellectual functioning is in a low range.

In the cases adopting categorical rules the Court has taken the following approach. The Court first considers objective indicia of society's standards, as expressed in legislative enactments and state practice to determine whether there is a national consensus against the sentencing practice at issue. Next, guided by the standards elaborated by controlling precedents and by the Court's own understanding and interpretation of the Eighth Amendment's text, history, meaning, and purpose, the Court must determine in the exercise of its own independent judgment whether the punishment in question violates the Constitution.

The present case involves an issue the Court has not considered previously: a categorical challenge to a term-of-years sentence. The analysis begins with objective indicia of national consensus. Seven jurisdictions permit life without parole for juvenile offenders, but only for homicide crimes. Thirty-seven States as well as the District of Columbia permit sentences of life without parole for a juvenile nonhomicide offender in some circumstances. Federal law also allows for the possibility of life without parole for offenders as young as 13. Relying on this metric, the State argues that there is no national consensus against the sentencing practice at issue. This argument is incomplete and unavailing. There are measures of consensus other than legislation. Here, an examination of actual sentencing practices in jurisdictions where the sentence in question is permitted by statute discloses a consensus against its use. Although these statutory schemes contain no explicit prohibition on sentences of life without parole for juvenile nonhomicide offenders, those sentences are most infrequent. According to a recent study, nationwide there are only 109 juvenile offenders serving sentences of life without parole for nonhomicide offenses.

Community consensus, while entitled to great weight, is not itself determinative of whether a punishment is cruel and unusual. In accordance with the constitutional design, the task of interpreting the Eighth Amendment remains our responsibility. The judicial exercise of independent judgment requires consideration of the culpability of the offenders at issue in light of their crimes and characteristics, along with the severity of the punishment in question. In this inquiry the Court also considers whether the challenged sentencing practice serves legitimate penological goals.

The Court has recognized that defendants who do not kill, intend to kill, or foresee that life will be taken are categorically less deserving of the most serious forms of punishment than are murderers. There is a line between homicide and other serious violent offenses against the individual. Serious nonhomicide crimes may be devastating in their harm but in terms of moral depravity and of the injury to the person and to the public, they cannot be compared to murder in their severity and irrevocability. This is because life is over for the victim of the murderer, but for the victim of even a very serious nonhomicide crime, life is not over and normally is not beyond repair. Although an offense like robbery or rape is a serious crime deserving serious punishment, those crimes differ from homicide crimes in a moral sense. It follows that, when compared to an adult murderer, a juvenile offender who did not kill or intend to kill has a twice diminished moral culpability. The age of the offender and the nature of the crime each bear on the analysis.

Life without parole is an especially harsh punishment for a juvenile. Under this sentence a juvenile offender will on average serve more years and a greater percentage of his life in prison than an adult offender. A 16-year-old and a 75-year-old each sentenced to life without parole receive the same punishment in name only. This reality cannot be ignored.

Penological theory is not adequate to justify life without parole for juvenile nonhomicide offenders. This determination; the limited culpability of juvenile nonhomicide offenders; and the severity of life without parole sentences all lead to the conclusion that the sentencing practice under consideration is cruel and unusual. This Court now holds that for a juvenile offender who did not commit homicide the Eighth Amendment forbids the sentence of life without parole.

ANALYSIS

Juvenile offenders cannot be sentenced to life without parole. Applying Eighth Amendment cruel-and-unusual-punishment principles, the Court held that there is no community consensus supporting such sentences and that they are unfair.

D. SILLY CRIMINAL STATUTES EXIST

Since legislatures can criminalize virtually anything they want to criminalize, there are a lot of—*how should I put this?*—unnecessary, outdated, or just plain silly crimes on the books. *See,* for example, the following:

- VA Code Ann. §18.2-156 ("If any person shall willfully and maliciously take or remove the waste or packing from any journal box of any locomotive, engine, tender, carriage, coach, car, caboose or truck used or operated upon any railroad, whether the same be operated by steam or electricity, he shall be guilty of a Class 6 felony.")
- 18 U.S.C.A. §711a ("Whoever, except as authorized under rules and regulations issued by the Secretary, knowingly and for profit manufactures, reproduces, or uses the character "Woodsy Owl", the name "Woodsy Owl", or the associated slogan, "Give a Hoot, Don't Pollute" shall be fined under this title or imprisoned not more than six months, or both.")
- 16 U.S.C.A. §4306(1) ("Any person who, without prior authorization from the Secretary knowingly destroys, disturbs, defaces, mars, alters, removes or harms any significant cave or alters the free movement of any animal or plant life into or out of any significant cave located on Federal lands, or enters a significant cave with the intention of committing any act described in this paragraph shall be punished in accordance with subsection (b) of this section.")

- 18 U.S.C.A. §711 ("Whoever, except as authorized under rules and regulations issued by the Secretary of Agriculture after consultation with the Association of State Foresters and the Advertising Council, knowingly and for profit manufactures, reproduces, or uses the character "Smokey Bear", originated by the Forest Service, United States Department of Agriculture, in cooperation with the Association of State Foresters and the Advertising Council for use in public information concerning the prevention of forest fires, or any facsimile thereof, or the name "Smokey Bear" shall be fined under this title or imprisoned not more than six months, or both.")

E. JUSTIFICATIONS FOR CRIMINAL PUNISHMENT

What *should* legislators be considering when they are deciding whether or not to criminalize some specific activity?

Certainly, one might logically argue, they *should* possess some sound justifications for imposing criminal punishment on previously innocent conduct since criminal convictions, unlike civil judgments, are dramatically stigmatizing. They affect, among other things, a convicted person's reputation, his or her status in society, personal relations, and career possibilities. Moreover, the commission of some serious crimes exposes the wrongdoer to the risk of imprisonment and/or substantial fines. Even when a criminal conviction carries only a nominal fine, the stigma of a criminal conviction is still there.

The Supreme Court has made the point that "punishment is justified under one or more of three principal rationales: rehabilitation, deterrence, and retribution." *Kennedy v. Louisiana*, 554 U.S. 407, 420, 128 S. Ct. 2641, 2649, 171 L. Ed.2d 525 (2009). And there are two types of deterrent justifications—general and specific (the latter is sometimes termed "restraint" or "incapacitation").

In brief, here is what we mean by using these common terms of art as justifications for criminalization and punishment:

- **Rehabilitation:** Criminalization based upon the idea of rehabilitation reflects the belief that convicted criminals can be "cured" during incarceration after conviction and then returned to society as they no longer pose a threat to others. The hope is that through appropriate treatment while confined, criminal offenders will be encouraged or trained to reenter society as productive citizens.
- **General Deterrence:** Criminalization based upon the idea of general deterrence reflects the belief that by punishing wrong-doers, society will benefit by keeping others from committing (deterring) the commission of future crimes. So, while specific deterrence focuses on

a specific convicted individual, general deterrence is intended to serve broader goals, acting as an example to other potential criminals about the risks of engaging in this kind of criminal behavior.

- **Specific Deterrence:** Criminalization based upon the idea of specific deterrence (also called "restraint" or "incapacitation") reflects the belief that criminal punishment is desirable in order to confine or isolate convicted criminals to prevent them from committing additional criminal acts. Additionally, the idea is that by punishing this particular ("specific") criminal, he or she will realize the seriousness of his or her antisocial behavior and will be deterred from committing future crimes as a result.

- **Retribution:** Criminalization based upon the idea of retribution reflects the belief that society *must* punish criminals because that is precisely what they deserve ("just deserts") or in order to exact vengeance for the wrongdoer's criminal acts. In the Old Testament of the Bible, this was called "an eye for an eye."

Appellate courts often analyze these very same traditional justifications for punishment in their application of the Cruel and Unusual Punishment Clause of the Eighth Amendment to the U.S. Constitution, as previously discussed in the *Graham* decision and in the following *Kennedy* decision.

CASE 18. Death sentence for rape of a child: In analyzing constitutional limitations on what a legislature can criminalize, courts often look to the traditional justifications for criminal punishment. As you can see from the *Kennedy* decision, the traditional justifications for punishment we have described can be and often are an important analytic tool for courts assessing the constitutionality of problematic criminal statutes. In the *Kennedy* case, the Court focused on general deterrence and retribution principles, finding as a result of that analysis that adults convicted of the nonhomicide crime of child rape cannot under the Eighth Amendment be sentenced to death.

PATRICK KENNEDY v. STATE OF LOUISIANA
554 U.S. 407, 128 S. Ct. 2641, 171 L. Ed.2d 525 (2008).

The Court: Patrick Kennedy seeks to set aside his death sentence under the Eighth Amendment. He was charged by the State of Louisiana with the aggravated rape of his then 8-year-old stepdaughter. After a jury trial, Kennedy was convicted and sentenced to death under a state statute authorizing capital punishment for the rape of a child under 12 years of age. This case presents the question whether the Constitution bars a state from imposing the death penalty for the rape of a child where the crime did not result, and was not intended to result, in death of the victim. We hold the Eighth Amendment prohibits the death penalty for this offense. The Louisiana statute is unconstitutional.

Our decision is consistent with the justifications offered for the death penalty. Capital punishment is excessive when it is grossly out of proportion to the crime or it does not fulfill the two distinct social purposes served by the death penalty: retribution and deterrence of capital crimes. Here it cannot be said with any certainty that the death penalty for child rape serves no deterrent or retributive function. This argument does not overcome other objections, however. The incongruity between the crime of child rape and the harshness of the death penalty poses risks of overpunishment and counsels against a constitutional ruling that the death penalty can be expanded to include this offense.

The goal of retribution, which reflects society's and the victim's interests in seeing that the offender is repaid for the hurt he caused, does not justify the harshness of the death penalty here. In measuring retribution, as well as other objectives of criminal law, it is appropriate to distinguish between a particularly depraved murder that merits death as a form of retribution and the crime of child rape.

There is an additional reason for our conclusion that imposing the death penalty for child rape would not further retributive purposes. In considering whether retribution is served, among other factors we have looked to whether capital punishment has the potential to allow the community as a whole, including the surviving family and friends of the victim, to affirm its own judgment that the culpability of the prisoner is so serious that the ultimate penalty must be sought and imposed. In considering the death penalty for nonhomicide offenses this inquiry necessarily also must include the question whether the death penalty balances the wrong to the victim.

It is not at all evident that the child rape victim's hurt is lessened when the law permits the death of the perpetrator. Capital cases require a long-term commitment by those who testify for the prosecution, especially when guilt and sentencing determinations are in multiple proceedings. In cases like this the key testimony is not just from the family but from the victim herself.

Society's desire to inflict the death penalty for child rape by enlisting the child victim to assist it over the course of years in asking for capital punishment forces a moral choice on the child, who is not of mature age to make that choice. The way the death penalty here involves the child victim in its enforcement can compromise a decent legal system; and this is but a subset of fundamental difficulties capital punishment can cause in the administration and enforcement of laws proscribing child rape.

With respect to deterrence, if the death penalty adds to the risk of nonreporting, that, too, diminishes the penalty's objectives. Underreporting is a common problem with respect to child sexual abuse. Although we know little about what differentiates those who report from those who do not report, one of the most commonly cited reasons for nondisclosure is fear of negative consequences for the perpetrator, a concern that has special force where the abuser is a family member. The experience of those who work with child victims indicates that, when the punishment is death, both the victim and the victim's family members may be more likely to shield the perpetrator from discovery, thus increasing underreporting. As a result, punishment by death may not result in more deterrence or more effective enforcement.

In addition, by in effect making the punishment for child rape and murder equivalent, a State that punishes child rape by death may remove a strong incentive for the rapist not to kill the victim. Assuming the offender behaves in a rational way, as one must to justify the penalty on grounds of deterrence, the penalty in some respects gives less protection, not more, to the victim, who is often the sole witness to the crime. It might be argued that, even if the death penalty results in a marginal increase in the incentive to kill, this is counterbalanced by a marginally increased deterrent to commit the crime at all. Whatever balance the legislature strikes, however, uncertainty on the point makes the argument for the penalty less compelling than for homicide crimes.

Each of these propositions, standing alone, might not establish the unconstitutionality of the death penalty for the crime of child rape. Taken in sum, however, they demonstrate the serious negative consequences of making child rape a capital offense. These considerations lead us to conclude, in our independent judgment, that the death penalty is not a proportional punishment for the rape of a child.

ANALYSIS

The Supreme Court held that a state cannot impose the death penalty for the rape of a child under the Eighth Amendment Cruel and Unusual Clause. The Court concluded that given the application of general deterrence and retribution principles, the incongruity between the crime of child rape and the harshness of the death penalty posed an unconstitutional risk of overpunishment.

The fact that Kennedy's sentence was overturned by the Supreme Court does not mean, however, that he was released. His conviction for the crime of child rape was not affected by this decision. Instead, the Court remanded his case to the Louisiana courts, where he was ultimately sentenced instead to life imprisonment at hard labor without benefit of parole, probation, or suspension of sentence.

F. THE SIGNIFICANCE OF THE MODEL PENAL CODE

Although every jurisdiction has the sovereign power to adopt its own Crimes Code with its own idiosyncratic set of criminal statues within the generous constitutional limits discussed above, there is nonetheless some general consistency in the way in which Congress and each of the states define the most serious of their criminal offenses.

There are two principal reasons for this:

- First, most U.S. criminal laws have the same Common Law origins, as discussed above; and
- second and equally important, most U.S. jurisdictions have adopted some or a good deal of the provisions contained in the ALI's MPC, briefly discussed in Chapter 6.

The ALI is the leading independent organization in the United States producing scholarly work to clarify, modernize, and otherwise improve the law. It is composed of 4,000 lawyers, judges, and law professors, all of whom are elected members, who draft, discuss, revise, and publish Restatements of the Law, model statutes, and principles of law that are enormously influential in the courts and legislatures, as well as in legal scholarship and education.

The MPC, a model Crimes Code, was adopted by the ALI in 1962. The MPC provisions are not precedential law in and of themselves. In fact, some MPC provisions were never adopted by any state, and others are outdated by now, especially the provisions relating to sex crimes.

But many states have enacted significant portions of the MPC as a part of their own Crimes Codes, and courts continue to refer to MPC provisions and commentary in interpreting criminal statutes. As a result, the MPC remains an important reference point for understanding Criminal Law in the United States.

More important still, at least from a practical viewpoint, your Criminal Law professor may often refer to MPC provisions when he or she is describing the differences in approach in a specific Criminal Law subject area between and among statutes criminalizing the same general behavior in different jurisdictions. This is what he or she is talking about—*not precedential law*, but model statutes that have often been adopted by (often many or most) individual state legislatures.

CHAPTER 9

Facts, Rules, and Applications in Criminal Decisions: The Importance of IRAC

A. THE IRAC FORMULA

You may get tired of hearing this, but most law professors will tell you time and time again: IRAC is the very best way to review, analyze, and prepare appellate court decisions for understanding them and for discussion in class.

It is true, as we have already discussed, that much of the mastery of Criminal Law revolves around *statutory* element analysis, not case law. *See* discussion in Chapter 6. Nonetheless, it is often true that in a Criminal Law class, the vehicle for prompting discussion of a particular criminal statute is an excerpt from an appellate court decision, a decision that focuses upon that statute's application in a specific set of factual circumstances.

Most of your homework assignments will involve reading appellate decisions like this, and the better you become at doing that, the quicker you will master the subject of Criminal Law. To be really good at reading and understanding what is in these case excerpts, you should use the IRAC approach.

So what is the IRAC formula?

IRAC is an acronym for the steps in analyzing a court's decision.

Issue → Rule → Analysis → Conclusion

More specifically:

Issue → The "issue" is a legal or factual question that the court is answering.

Rule → The "rule" is the specific rule of law that the court is applying to resolve (answer) the legal or factual question before the court. Sometimes, this "rule" may actually be standards or principles, however, and not a binding mandate like a statute. A "rule" hinges on one or two key facts, and all other facts are irrelevant. A "standard," in contrast, applies to a set of facts, none of which are determinative (as with a rule). And a "principle" does not really relate to particular facts at all, but is rather a value or goal to be pursued.

Analysis → The "analysis" is the court's discussion of precisely how the legal rule applies to the facts of the case before the court.

Conclusion → The "conclusion" is the answer to the "issue" (legal or factual question) that the court has addressed and results from the court's "analysis" (application of the legal "rule" to the facts of the case).

What you need to learn to do is to read appellate court decisions in criminal cases using an "IRAC frame of mind"; i.e., looking for and finding the Issues (there may be more than one issue), the Rules (there may be more than one of these, too), grasping the court's Analysis, and finally, figuring out just what the specific Conclusion is that the court has reached on that point.

There's a lot going on when you're in law school, to put it mildly, so you want to make sure to write your IRAC analysis down or type it into your computer, keeping it somewhere where it is easy to find and access quickly when you are in class and the case in question becomes the immediate topic for discussion. If you're the one called on to discuss this particular case, you don't want to waste even a second trying to find your IRAC analysis. You want, instead, to spend that time "showing off," demonstrating your awesome mastery of the IRAC points!

One more helpful (I hope) suggestion.

You should also record, right along with your IRAC case brief, a "shorthand" description of the facts in the case. Very short. Just a sentence fragment (like this sentence fragment). Nothing more.

The point of this shorthand is merely to help you remember exactly which case it is (out of the dozens you may have prepared for class discussion in all of your classes that week). I'm not talking about anything fancy or extensive. I'm suggesting that you use something like the "drunk driving road rage case," "constructive possession of weed case," "gross cruelty to animals case," or "burglary under duress case." You just need some very short, quick descriptors that will remind you—*quickly*—of the basic facts of that particular case; i.e., which one is it?

B. APPLYING IRAC

So how does this all work? Follow along with some appellate case examples to show you just how this works.

CASE 19. The jacking case: Using IRAC helps you better understand and prepare appellate court decisions for class discussion—is there sufficient evidence here? This *Davis* decision, which addresses the question of when a killing can be deemed to be first degree murder, is useful to demonstrate just how the IRAC analysis works.

STATE OF MISSOURI v. REGINALD DAVIS
905 S.W.2d 921 (Mo. Ct. App. 1995).

The Court: On the evening of Wednesday, December 2, 1992, Luther Blackwell, Demetrius Tabbs and Reginald Davis were drinking copiously of beer intermingled with gin. Tabbs drove them in his newly acquired car to the central west end of St. Louis. During the ride one of the others told Tabbs that they were going to "jack" somebody. When the car reached the vicinity of Euclid and Maryland Plaza, the group spied a couple on foot who turned out to be Natalie Hasty and Kevin Young. Davis and Blackwell left the car. Tabbs testified that Davis customarily carried a gun, which he concealed in the small of his back. He did not see him with the gun on this occasion, but did see Davis reach for the small of his back as he left the car.

Hasty and Young were unloading groceries from their car in the parking lot at the rear of an apartment on Maryland Plaza. Blackwell approached Hasty, flourished a knife, and demanded her purse. He then grabbed the purse and she tried to hold on to it. At the same time Davis headed toward Young. Just as soon as Hasty saw the person later identified as Davis, she noticed that he was carrying a handgun. Hasty heard the sound of chains rattling and assumed that Davis and Young were wrestling. She heard Davis say, "I want your money. Give me your wallet." Hasty then heard three shots. While she was thus distracted Blackwell escaped with her purse. She then went to Young, who was lying on the ground. Young was mortally wounded and died before arriving at the hospital.

Blackwell admitted the robbery, identifying Davis as his companion. He testified for the state after a plea bargain. Tabbs also was apprehended at his home and testified for the state.

Davis argues that the evidence does not establish the element of deliberation which is essential to a first degree murder conviction. Hasty testified, however, that Davis was carrying a handgun as he and Blackwell approached her and Young in the parking lot. The jury could have concluded that Davis had formed a deliberate purpose of using the gun during his criminal enterprise if necessary to accomplish his ends. Blackwell testified, furthermore, as follows:

And when I snatched her purse, I seen a black male dude. I mean a black male jump up out of the car and wrestle with Reginald [Davis]. And when he wrestled with Reginald, Reginald pulled the gun on him and shot him.

Davis therefore made a decision to use the weapon he was carrying when he was confronted by his intended robbery victim. This demonstrates deliberation.

The deliberation essential to a conviction of first degree murder need only be momentary. The instruction language, "cool reflection" might be applied by some jurors in a manner more favorable to Davis than the law strictly requires. The required reflection need be only momentary to establish deliberation.

Affirmed.

IRAC Analysis

Okay, first, how are you going to remember this case? There are some obvious ways to make up a shorthand reference here. Maybe you could just call this the "jacking case." That's what I did in the introduction to this case because I simply haven't read very many cases (none?) involving someone who said that he or she was trying to "jack" someone else.

When I've taught this case to first-year law students previously, a number of them were drawn to the description of "chains rattling." So maybe you'd just want to call this the "chain-rattling case." Or, if you're more of a purist, if you want something more descriptive of the crimes actually charged, you might call it "the groceries robbery/murder case." Key here is simply this: Pick something *short* that will serve as a reminder to you of the facts of the case; use the facts that jumped out at you when you read it to help you remember the entire factual scenario.

Now, on to the IRAC analysis itself. This is, you probably noticed, a pretty easy case to analyze in an IRAC fashion. They get harder. Much harder. But better to start with an easier one.

Hopefully, you recognized that the type of defense David raised was a failure-of-proof defense. *See* discussion in Chapter 7. The question that David raised with the appellate court was his claim that the prosecution failed in its proof of an essential element of first-degree murder. Specifically, Davis argued that the element that was not established sufficiently was the requirement that he acted with premeditation and deliberation.

What's the Issue here? Was there sufficient evidence introduced at trial from which the jury could have found that Davis acted with premeditation and deliberation in shooting Young?

What's the Rule here? As the court makes clear, to establish first-degree murder in Missouri under its statute, *inter alia*, the element of "deliberation" must be present. Put another way, the rule is that first-degree murder requires proof of deliberation beyond a reasonable doubt.

What's the Analysis here? Since the issue was the sufficiency of the prosecution's proof of an element, the court had to review the evidence produced at the trial to assess whether the evidence was sufficient for the jury to have reached its verdict of guilty. The court ruled that the evidence was sufficient to establish that Davis did in fact act with deliberation in shooting and killing Young because (1) Davis was carrying a gun when he engaged in the robbery; (2) the jury could infer from the facts that Davis intended to use that gun if necessary to help him complete the robbery; and (3) Davis made the decision to use the gun while he was wrestling with his victim.

What's the Conclusion here? Davis' first-degree murder conviction was affirmed because the court held that he acted with deliberation in shooting his victim.

Now, one more thing. And this is something that it would be wise to bear in mind *while* you are doing your IRAC analysis of an appellate court decision: Doing the IRAC analysis is a *necessary, but not sufficient, step* in preparing a case for a Criminal Law class. By that I mean to say that the IRAC framework is a good tool to prepare you to see and to describe the important features of the decision that you are analyzing. *But . . . it doesn't prepare you to assess the quality of that court's decision-making.* And you need to do that, too.

Let me explain what I mean by looking at the *Davis* decision again. The *Davis* Court held that the element of deliberation was sufficiently established to support a first-degree murder conviction. But the fact that the court reached that conclusion doesn't mean that it was correct. Oh, it's the law in Missouri after that decision. It's a correct statement of the law there. That much is clear. But was it the correct decision in a larger sense?

If second-degree murder in most jurisdictions is a reckless or impulsive killing (which it is) and first-degree murder is a killing undertaken with premeditation and deliberation (which it is), is it really so clear that, on these facts, Davis shot his victim after "deliberating" about it—*really?*—instead of merely acting recklessly or impulsively, which, granted, is a bad thing to do, but is not first-degree murder? Indeed, if the Davis case facts establish first-degree murder, can't virtually *any* otherwise impulsive killing be treated in much the same way, thereby blurring the line between first- and second-degree murder entirely?

For our purposes right now, without focusing on the substantive difference between these two types of murder (which you will talk about in a Criminal Law class), the point is only this: In addition to doing the IRAC analysis and figuring out exactly what is going on in the criminal decision under review, you should *also* be assessing the *quality* of the court's decision-making on each and every one of the IRAC framework points.

More specifically, let's look at each of the IRAC factors from a qualitative point of view, as follows:

Issue → Is the legal or factual question that the court is answering the right one? Is there a different question that the court should be addressing instead?

Rule → Is the specific rule of law that the court is applying to resolve (answer) the legal or factual question before the court the correct one? Is there a different rule that the court should be using instead?

Analysis → Is the court's discussion of precisely how the legal rule applies to the facts of the case before the court correct? Is the court missing something or is its analysis flawed in some way?

Conclusion → Is the court's answer to the issue that the court has addressed resulting from the court's analysis the correct one? Is there a better answer?

Certainly with respect to the court's analysis in the *Davis* decision, you will find in your Criminal Law course that not every jurisdiction agrees that there was enough of a factual basis for a jury to find the existence of deliberation beyond a reasonable doubt sufficient to support a verdict of first-degree murder. That doesn't mean that this court, the Missouri Court of Appeals, was wrong. It only means that other courts or other commentators might analyze the same rule on the same facts and come to an entirely different conclusion.

For your purposes right now, as a law student, what that means for you practically is that you can expect that if you were called on in class to "state the case" in *Davis*, you could not "get away" with merely having the IRAC analysis down pat. Oh, you would need to have done that and to know it, but you can also expect that your professor will be asking you to assess the quality of the court's decision-making as well, for example:

- Did it focus on the right Issue? (And if not, what issue *should* it have focused upon?)
- Did it use the right Rule? (And if not, what rule *should* it have used?)

- Was its analysis of that rule **A**ppropriate? (And if not, what *should* it have focused upon in its analysis?)
- Was its **C**onclusion the right one? (And, if not, what *should* it have concluded?)

Thinking about all of these points prior to class is, I concede, a lot of work to do with respect to each and every case you read for your Criminal Law class (and for your other classes as well). You need to apply the IRAC framework to each decision you study *and* you also need to assess the quality of the court's decision-making as to each and every one of those IRAC elements.

THE DRY-FIRING CASE

CASE 20. The dry-firing case: Using IRAC helps you better understand and prepare appellate court decisions for class discussion—is mens rea established? Let's go through another homicide case, this one involving the appeal of a second-degree murder conviction, using the IRAC framework once again.

STATE OF NEW HAMPSHIRE v. ARTHUR BURLEY
137 N.H. 286, 627 A.2d 98 (1993).

The Court: On January 7, 1989, Arthur Burley was at home with his ex-wife, Debbie Glines, with whom he had reconciled. At approximately 6:30 p.m., Burley telephoned 911 requesting an ambulance for a gunshot wound. The police and ambulance crews arrived to find Ms. Glines lying on the kitchen floor with a gunshot wound on the right side of her head, from which she eventually died.

Burley told the officers on the scene that he had been cleaning a .22 caliber semi-automatic handgun when it accidentally discharged. At the station, Burley explained that he had been keeping the handgun and a .22 caliber rifle for a friend. He stated that he retrieved the gun and a loaded clip of ammunition from a closet, placed them on tables in the living room, went to the kitchen for a beer, and took a cotton swab from the bathroom to clean the gun, which he admitted he had cleaned two weeks before. Burley loaded the gun, knowing he had made it ready to fire, before getting the beer. After watching television for twenty minutes, he picked up the gun and went to sit on the living room floor at the entryway to the kitchen. Burley knew that his ex-wife was in the kitchen. The gun went off, he stated, as he was cleaning excess oil from it, with the gun in his left hand and a finger in the trigger housing. Burley acknowledged familiarity with the operation of a .45 caliber semi-automatic, which is functionally similar to a .22.

A search of Burley's apartment revealed two spent bullet casings in a garbage bag. No cotton swabs were found in the living room or kitchen. Burley agreed to re-enact the shooting at his apartment. He admitted that he had occasionally "dry-fired" the gun by aiming the unloaded weapon at articles around the room.

Several days later, Burley returned to the police station and admitted, after being told of a bullet found lodged in his wall, that the second shell found in the trash came from Burley having fired the rifle in the apartment two days before shooting his ex-wife. Burley had been "joking around with it and it discharged." Ultimately, Burley admitted he had not been cleaning the handgun when he shot his ex-wife, although he denied he had been dry-firing it. Burley stated that he "was fooling around with it on the floor and it went off." In all, Burley gave the police three different versions of how he had been holding the gun that night.

Burley was tried on the charge of second degree murder. The indictment charged that the "defendant committed the crime of second degree murder by causing the death of his wife under circumstances manifesting an extreme indifference to the value of human life, by shooting her in the head with a pistol." Burley argues that the evidence was insufficient to prove the element of extreme indifference. We will uphold the verdict unless, viewing the evidence and all reasonable inferences in the light most favorable to the State, no reasonable trier of fact could have found guilt beyond a reasonable doubt. In a prosecution for second degree murder charging extreme indifference to the value of human life, the existence and extent of disregard manifested are for the jury to determine on the facts of the case.

The evidence here showed, *inter alia*, that Burley was familiar with the operation of a semi-automatic handgun, that Burley knew he had loaded the .22, and that Burley knew his ex-wife was in the next room. At the time of the shooting, Burley was sitting with his elbows resting on raised knees with the barrel of a gun he knew to be loaded pointing into the kitchen where his ex-wife was located. The gun was cocked and ready to fire, and Burley's finger was in the trigger housing. A firearms expert testified that due to its safety features the gun could not have fired without simultaneously gripping the safety on the back of the handle and squeezing the trigger. Burley, who had told the police he knew not to point a gun at anyone, finally admitted that he had been "fooling around" with it after consistently lying by saying he had been cleaning it. On all the evidence the jury was warranted in finding that Burley's conduct occurred under circumstances manifesting extreme indifference to the value of human life and in thereby finding him guilty of second degree murder.

IRAC ANALYSIS

How are you going to remember the facts of this case? Maybe you want to call this the "dry-firing case." (That's what most of my students have called it when I've taught this case to first-year law students in the past.) Trust me, in your entire law school career, you will never read many other cases that involve someone killing someone else while maybe (*he says he didn't do this . . . but do you believe him?*) "dry firing" his gun at her.

Now, let's do the IRAC analysis for this one. This decision is a bit less straightforward than *Davis*.

What's the Issue here? The overriding legal question here is whether Burley's second-degree murder jury conviction was erroneous. But the key to the answer to that question, given the legal rule set out immediately below, is whether the element of extreme indifference to the value of human life was established sufficiently to support a second-degree murder conviction in New Hampshire.

What's the Rule here? As the court makes clear, to establish second-degree murder in New Hampshire under its statute, *inter alia*, the element of "extreme indifference to the value of human life" must be proven by the prosecution. Put another way, the rule is that a second-degree murder conviction requires proof of extreme indifference to the value of human life beyond a reasonable doubt.

What's the Analysis here? The court found that the jury could reasonably have found that Burley acted with extreme indifference to the value of human life in shooting and killing his ex-wife because (1) he was familiar with the operation of the handgun and knew that his wife was in the kitchen; (2) he aimed the gun that he knew was loaded and ready to fire at the kitchen; (3) he admitted he was "fooling around" with the gun after lying to the police earlier about what he was doing with the gun; and (4) an expert had testified that the gun could not have been fired without simultaneously gripping the safety while pulling the trigger.

What's the Conclusion here? Burley's second-degree murder conviction was affirmed because the court held that the trial jury could reasonably have found on these facts that Arthur Burley acted with extreme indifference to the value of human life.

Once again, as with the *Davis* case discussed previously, in addition to simply using the IRAC framework to analyze this decision, you also need to assess the *quality* of the New Hampshire Supreme Court's decision-making. Using essentially the same grid as before, you want to ask yourself the following questions:

Issue → Was the legal or factual question that the *Burley* Court answered the right one? Is there a different question that the court should have addressed instead?

Rule → Was the specific rule of law that the court applied to resolve this legal or factual question before the court the correct one? Was there a different rule that the court should have used instead?

Analysis → Was the court's discussion of precisely how the legal rule applied to the facts of the case before the court correct, was the court missing something, or was its analysis flawed in some way?

Conclusion → Was the court's answer to the issue that the court was addressing resulting from the court's analysis, the correct one? Was there a better answer?

As you can see from the preceding discussion, the IRAC framework not only helps you analyze appellate decisions properly, but it also provides you with a useful and workable framework for assessing the quality of the conclusions that the court has reached in each of the four IRAC categories.

You will discover, moreover, that if you use the IRAC framework as set out above and look at each of these qualitative questions, it is certainly possible to use them to criticize aspects of the *Burley* Court's decision.

While most courts in most jurisdictions would likely have reached the same or a similar result on these facts, it is nonetheless true that some other courts would have applied different rules here (e.g., focusing only on whether Burley was reckless, not on extreme indifference), some courts might have engaged in a different analysis (e.g., finding insufficient evidence of extreme indifference), and, most important, surely, some courts may have reached a different conclusion (e.g., finding Burley's conduct to have "merely" been criminally negligent, not manifesting an extreme indifference to the value of human life sufficient to establish second-degree murder).

CASE 21. The child-luring case: Using IRAC helps you better understand and prepare appellate court decisions for class discussion—statutory interpretation. Take a look at another decision as another example of how to use the IRAC analysis. This one is a bit more complicated.

Try and apply the IRAC framework yourself. Do it before reading the discussion after the decision, which applies the framework for you. It doesn't take much time before you get the hang of it. Lawyers and judges have learned to do it as a simple matter of reflex.

COMMONWEALTH OF PENNSYLVANIA v. TERRENCE GALLAGHER
592 Pa. 262, 924 A.2d 636 (Pa. 2007).

The Court: The question presented in this appeal is whether the offense of luring a child, 18 Pa.C.S. §2910, is a strict liability crime with regard to the age of the victim.

At approximately 11:40 p.m. on August 3, 2002, 17-year-old M.N. was walking home from a convenience store. Terrence Gallagher stopped his car, asked M.N. for directions, and offered him a ride, which M.N. accepted. When Gallagher asked M.N. if he liked to drink, M.N. replied that he did. Gallagher then drove to a bar, bought beer, and took M.N. to his parked RV, where they began drinking. They then went to a second bar to purchase more beer. After returning to the RV, Gallagher performed oral sex on M.N.

Gallagher was charged with various crimes and following a bench trial, was found guilty of luring a child into a motor vehicle, 18 Pa.C.S. §2910: "A person who lures a child into a motor vehicle without the consent, express or implied, of the child's parent or guardian, unless the circumstances reasonably indicate that the child is in need of assistance, commits a misdemeanor of the first degree." Other statutory sections define "child" to mean a person under 18 years of age. M.N. was 17 years old when the incident occurred; therefore, he was a child under the statute.

Before the intermediate appellate court, Gallagher argued that because the trial court acquitted him of corruption of minors based specifically on his defense that he reasonably believed the complainant to be over the age of 18, such a factual finding precluded his conviction for luring a child into a motor vehicle in that the Commonwealth failed to prove that he possessed the sufficient mens rea to lure a person under the age of 18 into his car. The appeals court agreed, concluding that the Commonwealth had a duty to prove that Gallagher acted intentionally, knowingly, or at the very least, recklessly as to the complainant's age. Accordingly, the court concluded that the Commonwealth failed to sustain its burden with regard to the age element of §2910 and reversed the judgment of sentence on the luring conviction.

A plain reading of Section 2910 reveals that the statute does not express a mens rea requirement with regard to the age of the victim. The fact that a criminal statute is silent with regard to a culpability requirement does not mean that the Legislature intended to dispense with the same. There is a long-standing tradition that criminal liability is not to be imposed absent some level of culpability. This is because the imposition of absolute liability for a crime is generally disfavored and an offense will not be considered to impose absolute liability absent some indication of a legislative directive to dispense with mens rea. Therefore, the inquiry in this case is simply whether there is some indication of legislative intent to dispense with mens rea with regard to the age of the complainant in Section 2910.

We conclude that there is nothing in Section 2910 to indicate that the Legislature intended luring a child to be a strict liability crime regarding the age element. When the Legislature has intended that an offender is to be strictly liable for a crime regardless of his or her knowledge of the victim's age, it has done so explicitly. In the absence of a clear legislative directive to the contrary, we cannot ignore the long-standing tradition that criminal liability will not be imposed absent some level of mens rea.

For these reasons, the order of the appellate court reversing Gallagher's conviction is affirmed.

IRAC Analysis

How are you going to remember the facts of this case? What are you going to call it? What's *your* shorthand reference? Is this the "sex with the teen in the car case" to you? Or is the term "luring" more evocative for you, so you call it something like the "luring a child statute case"? Again, all you want to be able to do here is to create a quick shorthand that will serve as a memory spur to bring back all of the facts of this particular case. This shorthanding effort is not rocket science.

Now, let's do the IRAC analysis for the *Gallagher* decision. Again, you're best served if you try to do it yourself first before reading ahead.

What's the Issue here? First, the overriding claim here is whether the intermediate appellate court's reversal of Gallagher's conviction for luring a child into a motor vehicle (18 Pa.C.S. §2910) will stand? The key to answering this question is whether §2910 is a strict liability (termed "absolute liability" in this opinion) statute or, instead, whether it requires proof of the fact that the defendant *knew* that his victim was under the age of 18 (a fact the prosecution did not establish)?

What's the Rule here? As the Pennsylvania Supreme Court explained, a criminal statute that is silent about whether it contains a mens rea component (a specified criminal intention) will be deemed to require proof of a mens rea; i.e., it will *not* be deemed to be strict liability unless there is some express indication of a legislative intent to dispense with a mens rea requirement. More precisely, this is more of a principle than a rule, and the court is applying a standard based upon that principle.

What's the Analysis here? The court applied its policy of requiring an express indication from the legislature that it intended strict liability in order to dispense with mens rea in a criminal statute. In so doing, the court found that there was nothing in §2910 to indicate that the Legislature intended the crime of luring a child to be a strict liability crime. When the Legislature intends a crime to be strict liability, it states that position explicitly.

What's the Conclusion here? The Pennsylvania Supreme Court ruled that the statute required proof of a mens rea and the prosecution did not establish Gallagher's knowledge of the underage status of his victim beyond a reasonable doubt. Accordingly, the Pennsylvania Supreme Court affirmed the intermediate appellate court's reversal of Gallagher's conviction of luring a child into a motor vehicle.

Now let's assess the *qualitative* dimension of the *Gallagher* Court's decision-making using the IRAC framework as a guide:

Issue → Was the legal or factual question that the court answered the right one? Is there a different question that the court should have addressed instead?

Rule → Was the specific rule of law that the court applied to resolve this legal or factual question before the court the correct one? Was there a different rule that the court should have used instead?

Analysis → Was the court's discussion of precisely how the legal rule applied to the facts of the case before the court correct, was the court missing something, or was its analysis flawed in some way?

Conclusion → Was the court's answer to the issue that it was addressing resulting from the court's analysis, the correct one? Was there a better answer?

As with the prior two cases, other courts in other jurisdictions might certainly have reached different conclusions on each of these points. In all likelihood, some courts would probably have applied a different rule (test) for determining when the Legislature intended to enact a strict liability statute, for example. And some courts would certainly have concluded that there was sufficient evidence of such a legislative intent (strict liability) with a statute of this type.

But the point of your undertaking a qualitative assessment of any particular court's decision is not simply for you to be able to be in a position to approve or disapprove of the court's reasoning. Rather, the point is that a qualitative focus enables you to see not only what the court decided, but *how* it did it and why and how the decision-making might be different in a different jurisdiction, with a different statute, or with a modest change in the facts presented.

Rest assured, your Criminal Law professor will often be raising precisely these sorts of questions about the cases you are reading for your class. *Do your IRAC homework! Be prepared!*

CASE 22. Sex with the babysitter: Using IRAC helps you better understand and prepare appellate court decisions for class discussion—strict liability? One more example. This is another decision, like *Gallagher*, involving a question relating to statutory strict liability.

But in addition to applying the IRAC framework, you might also note when reading this next case just how different the approach of the Massachusetts Supreme Judicial Court is to strict liability issues, as compared to the approach taken by the Pennsylvania Supreme Court in the *Gallagher* decision.

COMMONWEALTH OF MASSACHUSETTS v. ANDRE KNAP
412 Mass. 712, 592 N.E.2d 747 (Mass. 1992).

The Court: Following a jury trial, Andre Knap was found guilty of rape of a child, and indecent assault and battery on a child under the age of fourteen. Knap appeals claiming that the trial judge erred when he refused to instruct the jury that a reasonable mistake of fact as to identity is a defense to charges of statutory rape and indecent assault and battery on a child. We affirm the convictions.

Knap testified that there was only one sexual episode between himself and the victim. One night in September of 1989, after he had taken his girlfriend to work and returned home, he went to bed for a nap which was his usual custom. He was awakened by someone massaging him, and then felt a hand go between his legs. The bedroom was kept very dark. He assumed his girlfriend was in bed with him. He responded by licking her breasts and "went between her legs" and "licked the outside of her vagina." He then realized that the person was not his girlfriend. He jumped up and turned on the light and saw the babysitter, who was naked. He knew she was thirteen years old. He told her to get out of the bed.

We have held that a reasonable mistake as to the age of the victim is not a defense to the crime of statutory rape. Knap argues that a reasonable mistake of fact as to identity, unlike a reasonable mistake of fact as to age, should be a defense to a charge of statutory rape and indecent assault and battery with a child under fourteen because if the facts were as Knap believed, he would have committed no crime. We see no reason to differentiate between a mistake as to age, and a mistake as to identity.

While the existence of a mens rea is the rule of, rather than the exception to, the principle of Anglo-American jurisprudence, it is just that—a general principle, not always a constitutionally mandated doctrine. States may create strict criminal liabilities by defining criminal offenses without any element of scienter.

Affirmed.

IRAC Analysis

You're not going to have any trouble finding a shorthand name for this particular decision, are you? Something like the "sex with the babysitter case" should bring these facts right back to you. I doubt you will be reading a lot of sex with the babysitter decisions. But, feel free to come up with a different shorthand reference if something works better for you. Shorthand these cases with whatever title brings the facts quickly to mind.

Now, let's do the IRAC analysis for the *Knap* decision. Once again, it would be a good idea if you tried to do this yourself before reading ahead.

What's the Issue here? The overriding legal question here is whether the convictions for Knap's rape of a child and indecent assault and battery on a child under the age of 14 should be affirmed or reversed? But the specific legal issue is whether Knap was entitled, as his attorney asked the trial judge, to have a reasonable mistake of fact as to identity defense instruction given to the trial jury based on Knap's testimony that he did not know his sex partner's identity?

What's the Rule here? The Massachusetts Supreme Judicial Court explains, albeit some of this implicitly, that there is no mistake defense possible to a strict liability offense; i.e., one that does not contain a scienter (state of mind) element.

What's the Analysis here? The court found that the two crimes for which Knap was convicted were both strict liability crimes simply by going through the statutory elements and finding that no scienter elements existed.

What's the Conclusion here? The trial court convictions were affirmed because Knap was not entitled to a reasonable mistake of fact as to identity instruction with respect to either charge as they were both strict liability offenses.

Finally, let's assess the *qualitative* dimension of the *Knap* Court's decision-making using the IRAC framework as a guide:

Issue → Was the legal or factual question that the *Knap* Court answered the right one? Is there a different question that the court should have addressed instead?

Rule → Was the specific rule of law that the court applied to resolve this legal or factual question before the court the correct one? Was there a different rule that the court should have used instead?

Analysis → Was the court's discussion of precisely how the legal rule applied to the facts of the case before the court correct, was the court missing something, or was its analysis flawed in some way?

Conclusion → Was the court's answer to the issue that the court was addressing resulting from the court's analysis, the correct one? Was there a better answer?

As with the prior three cases, other courts in other jurisdictions would certainly have reached different conclusions on each of these points. Some courts, for example, would most definitely have applied a different rule (test) for determining when the Legislature intended to enact a strict liability statute. In fact, that is exactly what happened in the very last decision, the *Gallagher* case. *Remember?*

In *Gallagher*, the court held expressly that "[i]n the absence of a clear legislative directive to the contrary, we cannot ignore the long-standing tradition that criminal liability will not be imposed absent some level of mens rea."

The *Knap* court didn't use this test. That's not a criticism of the *Knap* court, by the way. Every jurisdiction is perfectly free to use its own legal rules and tests. *See* discussion in Chapter 3. But the point is that if the *Gallagher* rule *had been* applied in the *Knap* case, the result may well have been, probably would have been, different.

By the way, that is just the sort of question your Criminal Law professor is prone to ask you, namely: "If the *Gallagher* rule had been applied in the *Knap* case, would the result have been different?" And vice versa, namely: "If the *Knap* rule had been applied in the *Gallagher* case, would the result have been different?"

Similarly, even using the same legal rule that the *Knap* court used, some courts might have concluded nonetheless that these statutes—although silent as to any applicable mens rea—did actually require a showing of scienter. (You will study some decisions just like this in your Criminal Law class when you are discussing the general subject of mens rea.)

In any event, do you see that by changing the Issue, the Rule, or the Analysis, the Conclusion a court might reach in any new decision could well be different? That's an important point. Using the IRAC framework as described in this chapter puts you in a position to discern and discuss the basis of a court's reasoning, assess that reasoning qualitatively, to respond to your Criminal Law professor's questions, and . . . look like a genius. What more could you ask for?

CHAPTER 10

The Importance of the Actus Reus and Mens Rea Elements

In Chapter 6, the focal role of element analysis in understanding and applying criminal statutes in the United States was discussed. Every element in a criminal statute is important, of course, as the prosecution has the burden of proving each and every one beyond a reasonable doubt.

But, that being said, there are nonetheless two elements of particular importance in criminal statutes—the actus reus (also called the criminal act) and the mens rea (also called the criminal intent). It is often said that a crime generally consists of the commission of a criminal act undertaken with criminal intent. More specifically, the *particular* actus reus and the *particular* mens rea that the Legislature has required as elements of a given crime must be proven by the prosecution.

A. THE ACTUS REUS ELEMENT

Every criminal statute should clearly state the specific criminal act (or acts) that is (or are) being criminalized. Or, sometimes, a criminal statute will describe instead an act that certain individuals are legally required to perform, e.g., a criminal statute might require doctors to report to the police that they have treated someone with a bullet wound or social workers to report to police evidence of child abuse. In these cases, the failure to perform a required act, deemed an "omission," is also considered a criminal act. These specified acts or failures to act are deemed to be the actus reus of the statute, the criminal act.

CASE 23. NYC gang killings: The commission of distinct criminal acts indicates the commission of distinct criminal offenses. This case involves a murder by shooting. Murder is a crime, of course; possession of an illegal weapon is also a crime. As the *Wright* case makes clear, the distinction between separate criminal acts can and often does make a *substantial* difference in the sentence that a convicted criminal defendant receives. In this case, defendant Ladarrius Wright received a 40-year sentence instead of a 25-year sentence, given the existence of separate and distinct actus reus elements in the two criminal offenses for which he was convicted.

PEOPLE OF THE STATE OF NEW YORK v. LADARRIUS WRIGHT
87 A.D.3d 229, 926 N.Y.S.2d 43 (2011).

The Court: Testimony at trial adduced the following: The murder of two young people in 2005 on West 133rd Street, Manhattan, occurred after a series of altercations between two groups of residents on the street. One group was comprised of Ladarrius Wright, his brother Curtis Wright and their friend Tamara Brown. The other group, reportedly members of the Bloods street gang, included the two victims, Doneil Ambrister and Yvette Duncan, who were shot as they walked along the street at approximately 1 A.M.

Trial testimony further established that, in the hours immediately prior to the shootings, the two groups were involved in an argument, and soon afterwards in a physical altercation in which Curtis Wright was struck in the forehead with a belt buckle. A few hours later, Ladarrius Wright approached Ambrister in the street as Ambrister walked back from a bodega with Duncan and several others. A witness for the People testified that Ladarrius Wright then said something to the effect of "So, I can't live on this block no more." Ambrister, Duncan and another member of the group, Mack Bruce, indicated they did not want to talk to Ladarrius, and started to walk away. Ladarrius Wright also appeared to be walking away. However, according to four witnesses who testified, instead of walking away, Ladarrius Wright drew a gun from his shorts. He then chased down Ambrister and shot him, fired at Duncan till she collapsed, and pointed the gun at Mack Bruce's head but the gun appeared to jam. Ambrister and Duncan died as a result of the shooting.

After a jury trial, Ladarrius Wright was convicted of one count of first-degree murder and second-degree criminal possession of a weapon. The court sentenced him to consecutive terms of 25 years to life for first-degree murder and 15 years on the weapon-possession conviction, for an aggregate term of 40 years to life. On appeal, Wright argues that the court erred in imposing consecutive sentences on the grounds that the People did not charge him with weapon possession unrelated to the murders.

Penal Law §70.25(2) mandates concurrent sentences "for two or more offenses committed through a single act or omission, or through an act or omission which in itself constituted one of the offenses and also was a material element of the other." Because both prongs of Penal Law §70.25(2) refer to an "act or omission," that is, to the actus reus that constitutes the offense, "the court must determine whether the actus reus element is, by definition, the same for both offenses . . . or if the actus reus for one offense is, by definition, a material element of the second offense."

The actus reus of a crime is the wrongful deed that comprises the physical components of a crime. The test, therefore, is not whether the criminal intent is one and the same and inspiring the whole transaction but whether separate acts have been committed with the requisite criminal intent.

The People correctly assert that the actus reus of the first-degree murder statute in this case is the causing of death of two or more persons with no requirement that it be by shooting, stabbing or any other method employing a weapon, and that the actus reus of second-degree criminal weapon possession is possession of a loaded operable firearm with no requirement that, in fact, it be employed in any way, much less lethally. Hence, these are separate and distinct acts.

Accordingly, the judgment of the Supreme Court, New York County, convicting defendant, after a jury trial, of murder in the first degree and criminal possession of a weapon in the second degree, and sentencing him to consecutive terms of 25 years to life and 15 years, respectively, should be affirmed.

ANALYSIS

Ladarrius Wright's *consecutive* sentences of 25 years to life for first-degree murder and 15 years for second-degree criminal weapon possession were affirmed because sentences must be concurrent *only* where they are based upon "a single act or omission." First-degree murder and second-degree criminal possession of a weapon have separate actus reus elements.

The actus reus of the first-degree murder is the causing of the death of two or more persons with no requirement that it be by shooting, stabbing, or any other method employing a weapon. The actus reus of second-degree criminal weapon possession is, in contrast, possession of a loaded operable firearm with no requirement that it be employed in any particular way.

B. THE MENS REA ELEMENT

In addition to the actus reus element, every criminal statute also contains—explicitly or implicitly—a specific culpable criminal intention or

mental state that the prosecution must prove beyond a reasonable doubt that the accused possessed in performing a forbidden criminal act in order to obtain a conviction for that crime. This is the mens rea element of the statute.

CASE 24. Iraq war protestor: The specific criminal intention required in a criminal statute must be established beyond a reasonable doubt in order to support a conviction. A criminal conviction will be reversed where the trial judge erroneously instructs the jury that it can or should assess the accused person's culpability on the basis of a *lesser* showing of criminal intention than the statute actually requires. As a perfect example of this proposition, consider the Vermont Supreme Court's decision and analysis in *Jackowski*, set out below, a case involving an antiwar protester who blocked traffic at the main intersection in town.

STATE OF VERMONT v. ROSEMARIE JACKOWSKI
181 Vt. 73, 915 A.2d 767, 2006 VT 119 (2006).

The Court: Rosemarie Jackowski was arrested on March 20, 2003, during an antiwar demonstration at the intersection of Routes 7 and 9 in Bennington. During the demonstration, protesters blocked traffic at the intersection for approximately fifteen minutes. Jackowski stood in the intersection, praying and holding a sign bearing anti-war slogans and newspaper clippings, including an article accompanied by a photograph of a wounded Iraqi child. Police officers repeatedly asked Jackowski to leave the intersection, and when she refused, she was arrested, along with eleven other protesters. The State charged them with disorderly conduct, alleging that Jackowski and the other protesters, "with intent to cause public inconvenience and annoyance, obstructed vehicular traffic, in violation of 13 V.S.A. §1026(5)."

Jackowski's intent was the only issue contested during her one-day jury trial. After several police officers testified for the State, Jackowski took the stand, admitting to blocking traffic, but stating that her only intention in doing so was to protest the war in Iraq, not to cause public inconvenience or annoyance. At the conclusion of the trial, the court first instructed the jury that the State could establish Jackowski's intent to cause public inconvenience or annoyance by proving beyond a reasonable doubt that she acted "with the conscious object of bothering, disturbing, irritating, or harassing some other person or persons." The court then added, "This intent may also be shown if the State proves beyond a reasonable doubt that the defendant was practically certain that another person or persons ... would be bothered, disturbed, irritated, or harassed." The jury convicted Jackowski of disorderly conduct.

Jackowski argues that the jury charge was improper because the trial court failed to instruct the jury to consider whether she acted with the requisite criminal intent. Jackowski relies on *State v. Trombley* to draw a distinction between offenses that require purposeful or intentional misconduct and those that require only knowing misconduct. In *Trombley*, we held that it was error for the trial court to instruct the jury to consider whether the defendant in an aggravated assault case acted "knowingly" or "purposely," when he was charged with "purposely" causing serious bodily injury. A person acts "purposely" when "it is his conscious object to engage in conduct of that nature or to cause such a result." A person acts "knowingly" when "he is aware that it is practically certain that his conduct will cause such a result."

Jackowski argues that *Trombley* controls here, as the trial court used a similarly worded jury charge. The State cites several cases supporting the proposition that both "purposely" and "knowingly" causing harm involve some element of "intent," and thus, that *Trombley's* distinction between "purposely" and "knowingly" is illusory. Each of these cases predates our decision in *Trombley*, however, and each adheres to an outmoded distinction between "specific intent" and "general intent" crimes—the distinction that the Legislature rejected in adopting the Model Penal Code's approach to mens rea. It was therefore error for the trial court to charge the jury to consider whether Jackowski was "practically certain" that her actions would cause public annoyance or inconvenience.

Intent was the only issue Jackowski contested at trial. Jackowski claimed that she intended only to protest the war in Iraq, not to cause public annoyance or inconvenience. The State is correct that Jackowski could have had multiple intents, and a jury could certainly have convicted Jackowski based on the evidence presented at trial. The law makes a distinction between intentional and knowing acts, however, and Jackowski was entitled to have a jury decide whether causing public annoyance or inconvenience was her conscious object. The trial court's instruction prevented the jury from considering that question, effectively removing the element of intent from the crime, if not directing a guilty verdict. We cannot say that this error was harmless beyond a reasonable doubt, so we must reverse Jackowski's conviction.

ANALYSIS

Jackowski's conviction was reversed because the trial judge instructed the jury that it could convict her of the crime of disorderly conduct if she was "practically certain that another person or persons ... would be bothered, disturbed, irritated, or harassed" by her actions. This instruction was erroneous because the disorderly conduct statute itself contained a mens rea element of intentional conduct, which would only be satisfied if the prosecution showed that her "conscious object" was to bother, disturb, irritate, or harass another person.

As you can see from the *Jackowski* decision, a criminal conviction cannot stand if the jury has been instructed that it can or should apply the wrong—lower and easier to prove—mens rea.

But ... it's a lawyer's job to follow a court's reasoning closely, to look beyond the bottom-line conclusion—in this case, the reversal of Rosemary Jackowski's conviction. In doing that, you can quickly see that the *Jackowski* decision and the Vermont Supreme Court's holding in that case does *not* mean that the court found that Jackowski did not possess the required mens rea required under the disorderly conduct statute. Instead, the court found *only* that the court misinstructed the jury.

Why is that important?

It's important because in a retrial, it is perfectly possible, if not altogether likely, that the next (properly instructed) jury would find that Ms. Jackowski had what the prosecution called "multiple intents," i.e., she intended to protest the war in Iraq but that she *also* intended to bother, disturb, irritate, or harass the motorists who could not drive through the intersection that she blocked.

Indeed, the court predicted as much, noting that "a jury could certainly have convicted defendant based on the evidence presented at trial." Moreover, a dissenting justice in the *Jackowski* case made this point even more directly: "That defendant was also motivated by a noncriminal urge to communicate and show political opposition does not mutually exclude a contemporaneous and, in this case, manifest criminal intent to cause public inconvenience and annoyance."

C. STRICT LIABILITY OFFENSES

It is important to add that there is an important exception to this general rule—that every criminal statute contains a mens rea element. Sometimes a criminal statute will be deemed to be "strict liability," i.e., it applies to commission of the proscribed offense without reference to any particular culpable mental state. In that case, the prosecution need not prove any criminal intention at all on the part of the accused in order to convict under that statute; proof of the actus reus—and any additional elements described in the statute—is enough to convict.

But, as you will discuss in your Criminal Law class, strict liability is not the norm, at least not for serious criminal offenses. The traditional view is that a person should not be convicted of a serious criminal offense unless he or she possesses an appropriately blameworthy criminal intention.

Usually, the "higher" the mens rea (the more difficult it is to prove), the more serious the criminal offense and the potential criminal penalty. First-degree murder, for example, usually requires proof of a killing act (the actus reus) committed *purposely* or *intentionally*, which is a very difficult mental state to prove beyond a reasonable doubt. But negligent homicide, in contrast—a less serious offense—requires proof "only" of a killing act committed while the accused acted with criminal negligence, which is a far less difficult mental state for the prosecution to prove to the satisfaction of a jury.

D. ADDITIONAL CIRCUMSTANTIAL ELEMENTS

In addition to a mens rea (or strict liability) and an actus reus, many criminal statutes also contain one or more additional elements that relate to particular circumstances that must be proved by the prosecutor for the particular crime to be made out.

For example, consider a New Jersey statute, N. J. S. A. 2C:12-10(e), which provides that "[a] person is guilty of a crime of the third degree if he commits the crime of stalking while serving a term of imprisonment or while on parole or probation as the result of a conviction for any indictable offense under the laws of this State, any other state or the United States."

The actus reus in this statute is the act of "stalking." ("Stalking," by the way, is elsewhere defined in the New Jersey statutes as "purposefully or knowingly engag[ing] in a course of conduct directed at a specific person that would cause a reasonable person to fear for his safety or the safety of a third person or suffer other emotional distress.")

But, in addition to proving that actus reus, to make out a violation of N. J. S. A. 2C:12-10(e), a prosecutor would also have to prove beyond a reasonable doubt an *additional circumstantial element*, namely that the accused was "serving a term of imprisonment or [was] on parole or probation as the result of a conviction for any indictable offense under the laws of [New Jersey], any other state or the United States."

E. ASCERTAINING THE ACTUS REUS AND MENS REA ELEMENTS

It is not terribly difficult, in the typical case at least, to figure out which elements in a criminal statute are the actus reus and which are the mens rea elements.

Consider, for example, Alaska's first-degree arson statute, Alas. Stat. §11.46.400 (a):

A person commits the crime of arson in the first degree if the person intentionally damages any property by starting a fire or causing an explosion and by that act recklessly places another person in danger of serious physical injury.

The actus reus? Damaging any property by starting a fire or causing an explosion that places another person in danger of serious physical injury.

The mens rea? Actually, as you can see, there are two of them. The prosecution must prove that act of damaging property by starting a fire or causing an explosion was *intentional*, and the prosecution must also prove that the act of placing another person in danger of serious physical injury was (at least) *reckless*.

Different mens rea elements are often enacted for different actus reus elements. Even in the same statute. This is not at all uncommon.

Moreover, a criminal statute may also contain a number of different actus reus and/or mens rea elements, which may be proved by the prosecution *in the alternative*. What do I mean by that? The point is simply that the prosecution need not prove each and every element when they are stated in such a way that proof only of one or the other will suffice, i.e., the prosecution (and the jury) may choose from the different elements.

An example should, hopefully, make this clearer. Consider Pennsylvania's robbery statute, 18 Pa. C. S. §3701(1), which provides as follows:

A person is guilty of robbery if, in the course of committing a theft, he

(i)   inflicts serious bodily injury upon another;
(ii) threatens another with or intentionally puts him in fear of immediate serious bodily injury;
(iii) commits or threatens immediately to commit any felony of the first or second degree;

(iv) inflicts bodily injury upon another or threatens another with or intentionally puts him in fear of immediate bodily injury;

(v) physically takes or removes property from the person of another by force however slight; or

(vi) takes or removes the money of a financial institution without the permission of the financial institution by making a demand of an employee of the financial institution orally or in writing with the intent to deprive the financial institution thereof.

Do you see the number of *different* types of robbery that the prosecution might establish, each with a different requisite actus reus and mens rea element? Once the commission of a theft has been proven, the greater offense of robbery can be proven by showing that the accused

- inflicted serious bodily injury upon another person (an actus reus element with no mens rea);
- threatened another person with or intentionally put another person in fear of immediate serious bodily injury (alternate actus reus elements with no mens rea);
- committed or threatened immediately to commit any felony of the first or second degree (alternate actus reus elements with no mens rea);
- committed or threatened immediately to commit any felony of the first or second degree (alternate actus reus elements with no mens rea);
- inflicted bodily injury upon another or threatened another with or intentionally put another person in fear of immediate bodily injury (three alternate actus reus elements, two with no mens rea and one—the last—with a mens rea of an "intentional" mental state);
- physically took or removed property from the person of another person by force however slight (an actus reus element with no mens rea); or
- took or removed the money of a financial institution without the permission of the financial institution by making a demand of an employee of the financial institution orally or in writing with the intent to deprive the financial institution thereof.

You see? This is only one statute, only one crime: Robbery. But this one statute nonetheless contains a number of different (alternative) ways to prove the same crime by means of proof of at least one of the actus reus elements described, one with a requisite mens rea element and the rest of them without one.

Consider finally as another and even more sophisticated example of parsing actus reus and mens rea elements, the following portion of a criminal homicide statute, first-degree murder, taken from California Penal Code §189:

> All murder which is perpetrated by means of a destructive device or explosive, a weapon of mass destruction, knowing use of ammunition designed primarily to penetrate metal or armor, poison, lying in wait, torture, or by any other kind of willful, deliberate, and premeditated killing, or which is committed in the perpetration of, or attempt to perpetrate arson, rape, carjacking, robbery, burglary, mayhem, kidnapping, train wrecking, . . . , or any murder which is perpetrated by means of discharging a firearm from a motor vehicle, intentionally at another person outside of the vehicle with the intent to inflict death, is murder of the first-degree.

What is the actus reus, the criminal act, that is proscribed by this statute?

Than answer is that it is the act of "murder." But, as you can see from the fragment of the statute set out above, "murder" is not defined expressly in that text. If a statute does not define important element terms, in our common law system of adjudication, you need to look at the case law, the precedent, in that jurisdiction to see how the courts may have defined that term. Typically and unsurprisingly, the act of murder is defined simply as "a killing act."

What is the mens rea, the criminal intention, that is proscribed by this statute?

The answer to this question is a bit more complicated because this statute has different mens rea provisions for each of the different criminal acts comprising the crime of first-degree murder in California.

There is, as you can see, no express mens rea at all provided for the murderous acts of killing by means of a destructive device or explosive, a weapon of mass destruction, poison, lying in wait, or torture. Nor is there an express mens rea provided for killings that occur in the perpetration of, or attempt to perpetrate, arson, rape, carjacking, robbery, burglary, mayhem, kidnapping, or train wrecking.

But . . . a killing by use of ammunition designed primarily to penetrate metal or armor must be committed "knowingly." Do you see that in the statute? Look at it again. That particular act does have a prescribed mens rea: *Knowingly.*

Moreover, this same statute also punishes murderous acts that were committed with a different mens rea, namely any and all willful, deliberate, and premeditated killings. The fact that the accused acted willfully, with premeditation and deliberation, is a quite different thing for a prosecutor to have to prove than just showing that the accused committed a murderous act by shooting someone with armor-piercing ammunition and did that "knowingly." A different mens rea is provided for a different actus reus. Do you see?

And there's yet another mens rea still in this statutory fragment. The last clause adds "any murder which is perpetrated by means of discharging a firearm from a motor vehicle, intentionally at another person outside of the vehicle with the intent to inflict death" as first-degree murder as well. Do you see the mens rea provision in this clause?

To convict an accused person under this part of this statute, the prosecution would have to establish beyond a reasonable doubt, *inter alia*, that the accused killer shot his or her victim from a motor vehicle, *intentionally* aiming at the victim and with the further *intent* to cause the victim's death. To convict someone under this part of the first-degree murder statute then the accused person's mens rea of intentional conduct must be established.

What additional circumstantial elements—beyond the actus reus and mens rea—are included in this statute?

Well, as you can see, there are quite a lot of them. Just for example:

- To establish first-degree murder as a result of a killing act "committed in the perpetration of, or [an] attempt to perpetrate arson, rape, carjacking, robbery, burglary, mayhem, kidnapping, train wrecking," the prosecution has to establish beyond a reasonable doubt, *inter alia*, that one of the listed felonies was committed by the accused, during the perpetration of which, the victim was killed.
- To establish first degree murder as a result of a killing act that was "perpetrated by means of discharging a firearm from a motor vehicle, intentionally at another person outside of the vehicle with the intent to inflict death," the prosecution has to establish beyond a reasonable doubt, *inter alia*, that the accused (1) used a firearm, (2) discharged that firearm from a motor vehicle, and (3) aimed at a person outside of the vehicle.

With respect to that latter example—shooting someone from a car—note the importance of each and every one of the elements in establishing the commission of this particular crime. If an accused was the driver of a car, aimed at, shot, and killed one of his passengers, he is not guilty . . . at least of this part of the first degree murder statute. The passenger was inside the car and the circumstantial elements set out in the statute apply only to cases where the victim aimed at was *outside* of the car.

Query, however, whether this shooter might be successfully tried and convicted under some other part of this first-degree murder statute. *What do you think?*

CASE 25. Aggravated identity theft: It is important to determine which actus reus element a particular mens rea element modifies. Figuring out which actus reus element a particular mens rea element modifies is, however, not always easy. The following Supreme Court decision, *Flores-Figueroa v. United States*, illustrates that point perfectly. Even the justices of the United States Supreme Court had to struggled with the question of what the defendant had to know at the time he acted in order to satisfy the statute. So don't feel bad if you find this topic a bit difficult as well.

IGNACIO CARLOS FLORES-FIGUEROA v. UNITED STATES
556 U.S. 646, 129 S.Ct. 1886, 173 L.Ed.2d 853 (2009).

The Court: A federal criminal statute forbidding "[a]ggravated identity theft" imposes a mandatory consecutive 2-year prison term upon individuals convicted of certain other crimes if, during (or in relation to) the commission of those other crimes, the offender "knowingly transfers, possesses, or uses, without lawful authority, a means of identification of another person." 18 U.S.C. §1028A(a)(1). The question is whether the statute requires the Government to show that the defendant knew that the "means of identification" he or she unlawfully transferred, possessed, or used, in fact, belonged to "another person." We conclude that it does.

Ignacio Flores-Figueroa is a citizen of Mexico. In 2000, to secure employment, Flores gave his employer a false name, birth date, and Social Security number, along with a counterfeit alien registration card. The Social Security number and the number on the alien registration card were not those of a real person. In 2006, Flores presented his employer with new counterfeit Social Security and alien registration cards; these cards (unlike Flores' old alien registration card) used his real name. But this time the numbers on both cards were in fact numbers assigned to other people. The United States charged Flores with aggravated identity theft, 18 U.S.C. §1028A(a)(1), the crime at issue here.

Flores moved for a judgment of acquittal on the "aggravated identity theft" count. He claimed that the Government could not prove that Flores knew that the numbers on the counterfeit documents were numbers assigned to other people. The Government replied that it need not prove that knowledge. After a bench trial, the court found Flores guilty of the predicate crimes and aggravated identity theft.

There are strong textual reasons for rejecting the Government's position. As a matter of ordinary English grammar, it seems natural to read the statute's word "knowingly" as applying to all the subsequently listed elements of the crime. The Government cannot easily claim that the word "knowingly" applies only to the statute's first four words, or even its first seven. It makes little sense to read the provision's language as heavily penalizing a person who "transfers, possesses, or uses, without lawful authority," a something, but does not know, at the very least, that the "something" (perhaps inside a box) is a "means of identification." Would we apply a statute that makes it unlawful "knowingly to possess drugs" to a person who steals a passenger's bag without knowing that the bag has drugs inside? The Government claims more forcefully that the word "knowingly" applies to all but the statute's last three words, i.e., "of another person." The statute, the Government says, does not require a prosecutor to show that the defendant knows that the means of identification the defendant has unlawfully used in fact belongs to another person. But how are we to square this reading with the statute's language?

In ordinary English, where a transitive verb has an object, listeners in most contexts assume that an adverb (such as knowingly) that modifies the transitive verb tells the listener how the subject performed the entire action, including the object as set forth in the sentence. Thus, if a bank official says, "Smith knowingly transferred the funds to his brother's account," we would normally understand the bank official's statement as telling us that Smith knew the account was his brother's.

Of course, a statement that does not use the word "knowingly" may be unclear about just what Smith knows. Suppose Smith mails his bank draft to Tegucigalpa, which (perhaps unbeknownst to Smith) is the capital of Honduras. If the bank official says, "Smith sent a bank draft to the capital of Honduras," he has expressed next to nothing about Smith's knowledge of that geographic identity. But if the official were to say, "Smith knowingly sent a bank draft to the capital of Honduras," then the official has suggested that Smith knows his geography.

Similar examples abound. If a child knowingly takes a toy that belongs to his sibling, we assume that the child not only knows that he is taking something, but that he also knows that what he is taking is a toy and that the toy belongs to his sibling. If we say that someone knowingly ate a sandwich with cheese, we normally assume that the person knew both that he was eating a sandwich and that it contained cheese.

The manner in which the courts ordinarily interpret criminal statutes is fully consistent with this ordinary English usage. That is to say courts ordinarily read a phrase in a criminal statute that introduces the elements of a crime with the word "knowingly" as applying that word to each element. We conclude that §1028A(a)(1) requires the Government to show that the Flores knew that the means of identification at issue belonged to another person.

ANALYSIS

Flores's conviction for aggravated identity theft was reversed because the prosecution did not prove that he "knew" that he was using the means of identification of another person. The Court held that this mens rea term modified *all* of the elements of the aggravated identity theft statute, not just the accused's knowledge that he was "using" a false identity document.

The explicit text of the statute supported this interpretation. And the Court also held that generally criminal statutes that introduce the elements of a crime with the word "knowingly" apply that mens rea term of art to each element of the offense.

CHAPTER 11

Focusing on Appellate Decisions in Criminal Cases

A. THE CASE METHOD

Most Criminal Law classes in the United States are taught using the "case method" of instruction. What that means, essentially, is that the primary course text you are likely to use in your class will be a "casebook," a collection of heavily edited appellate decisions ("cases"), each of which is included in order to illustrate—and spur discussion of—one or more specific legal points.

These cases will ordinarily begin by describing the underlying facts at issue in each case, and then they will discuss a number of legal issues that have been raised by counsel for a convicted defendant, now called the appellant (or sometimes the petitioner), on appeal. (The prosecution is not allowed to appeal a verdict of acquittal due to the constitutional protection against double jeopardy, so you will rarely come across a case in your casebook where the Government is the appellant. The Government is usually the party called the "appellee.")

B. ISSUES RAISED ON APPEAL

Often the issues raised on appeal by the appellant involve the application of the language of particular criminal statutes to the facts of the case. These issues will commonly involve, for example, questions of

- whether the trial judge instructed the jury accurately on one or more elements of a charged offense;
- whether the trial judge instructed the jury accurately (or at all) on one or more elements of a defense raised by the defendant;
- whether the trial judge failed to instruct the jury on a defense that the defendant wanted but was not permitted to raise;
- whether the trial judge erred in making an evidentiary ruling;

- whether the conviction on a particular charge was supported by the evidence that came in at trial; and
- whether the conviction on a particular charge was supported by the weight of the evidence introduced at trial.

CASE 26. Rape of a prostitute: No criminal trial is perfect—the ultimate question on appeal is, "Was the trial fair?" As you are discovering or as you will discover while in law school, there is a lot that goes into prosecuting and defending a criminal case. Prosecutors and defense counsel must each make quick, split-second decisions of great importance to the outcome of the proceedings. These include tactical and strategic decisions about which defenses to pursue or how to respond to those defenses, decisions about what evidence or witnesses to introduce and how to respond to that evidence or those witnesses, and decisions about when and whether to object to actions of opposing counsel or the trial judge. In this setting, there are many, many opportunities for missteps and errors to occur, not only on counsels' part, but also by the trial judge.

That said, the ultimate issue on appeal is not, *Was there an error committed at trial?* There is almost always an error, if not many errors. The ultimate question, in contrast, is a more fundamental one—whether the trial proceedings were fair. As one federal court has observed, "there are many fair trials but few perfect ones." *U.S. v. Raineri*, 42 F.3d 36, 45 (1st Cir. 1994).

That was the question the Appeals Court of Massachusetts focused upon in the *Enimpah* decision, namely, "Was Enimpah's trial fair?"

COMMONWEALTH OF MASSACHUSETTS v. BRIAN ENIMPAH
81 Mass. App. Ct. 657, 966 N.E.2d 840 (2012).

The Court: The jury heard evidence that the victim was a sex worker who initially agreed to sexual intercourse with Brian Enimpah for a fee. During intercourse, according to the victim's testimony, Enimpah became very aggressive and forceful. When she asked him to slow down, "he started becoming more aggressive." She tried to squirm away, telling him to stop, that this was not what was arranged; in response, he "put more weight on top of [her], and wrapped his arm around [her] two arms and put his hand over [her] mouth" so that she could not scream. Enimpah's weight restrained her so that she "couldn't fight him off." Afterwards, as she was crying and in pain, he took the money he had paid her from her pants pockets and left.

During the instructions at the end of the case, the judge told the jury: "Rape is natural sexual intercourse with another person by force and against that person's will, or that compels a person to submit to such an act by threat of bodily force or violence . . . .' 'Natural intercourse' . . . consists of inserting the penis into the female sex organ. Natural sexual intercourse is complete upon penetration, no matter how slight, of a person's genital opening . . . . The [C]ommonwealth must prove that at the time of penetration the complainant did not consent, or in other words that the intercourse was against the complainant's will."

Enimpah argues that the jury could not reasonably have found him guilty of rape. He does not suggest that consent may not be withdrawn during intercourse or that the facts themselves are insufficient to support a charge of rape. Rather, he argues that "at no point did the judge tell the jury that intercourse could become rape if the [victim] consented to being penetrated."

The Massachusetts rape statute follows the common-law definition of rape, and requires the Commonwealth to prove beyond a reasonable doubt that the defendant committed (1) sexual intercourse (2) by force or threat of force and against the will of the victim. As to the first element, there has been very little disagreement. Sexual intercourse is defined as penetration of the victim, regardless of degree.

Enimpah reads the judge's language too narrowly. The instruction that "[t]he [C]ommonwealth must prove that at the time of penetration the complainant did not consent," was immediately followed by the clarifying language "or in other words that the intercourse was against the complainant's will." These instructions accurately described for the jury the elements of the crime of rape and cannot reasonably be read to exclude the facts of this case. Here, there was evidence that the victim consented at the time of the initial penetration, but withdrew her consent during the subsequent intercourse. Enimpah then forcibly continued to have intercourse with her, despite her pleas for him to stop and her efforts to get away from him. If the jury believed that evidence, the judge's instructions permitted them to find Enimpah guilty of rape. We see no error, and there was no substantial risk of a miscarriage of justice.

ANALYSIS

Enimpah's conviction for rape was affirmed because the instructions given to the jury were, in the appellate court's view, fair and accurate. Enimpah argued that the trial judge misinstructed the jury by not telling them *expressly* that intercourse could become rape if the victim initially consented but subsequently withdrew her consent. But the appellate court disagreed, finding that the trial judge's instructions made the point sufficiently, that intercourse must *always* be consensual, without the necessity of the judge having to say anything more specific about the law than that.

CASE 27. Shooting in the apartment complex: No criminal trial is perfect—the ultimate question on appeal is, "Was the trial fair?" The trial judge's instruction in *Kendrick* was not perfect. But again, perfection is not what appellate courts require in the criminal trial proceedings they review. The Georgia Supreme Court concluded that despite any arguable instructional error, Kendrick was convicted of felony murder in a fair trial.

MICHAEL KENDRICK v. STATE OF GEORGIA
290 Ga. 873, 725 S.E.2d 296 (Ga. 2012).

The Court: On May 21, 2001, Michael Kendrick, Timothy Copeland, and several other men, including Anthony Willoughby and Carl Tucker, were drinking outside Chapel Forest Apartments in Fulton County. An altercation arose between Kendrick and Copeland, and Kendrick struck Copeland in the head with a gin bottle and poured beer on him. The fight was broken up, and Kendrick and Anthony Willoughby left the premises to buy more beer. In the meantime, Copeland went home to change his shirt and returned to the gathering. Shortly thereafter, Willoughby drove up in his car with Kendrick in the passenger seat. Two eyewitnesses saw Kendrick get out of the car and start shooting at Copeland. Copeland began running, but he was struck by a bullet and fell on the ground. Kendrick reloaded, and, according to the two eyewitnesses, stood over the fallen Copeland and shot him in the back. Both eyewitnesses testified that Copeland was unarmed, and testing of Copeland's hands indicated that he had not fired a gun. Kendrick fled after the shooting, and Copeland died at the scene from the gunshot wounds.

These facts were sufficient to enable the jury to find Kendrick guilty of the crime of felony murder beyond a reasonable doubt. Although Kendrick and Willoughby testified that Copeland began shooting at Kendrick first, the jury, as the arbiter of witness credibility, was entitled to disbelieve this version of the facts.

Kendrick argues that the trial court gave the jury an incomplete charge regarding the lesser included offense of voluntary manslaughter. The record shows that the trial court charged the jury:

With regard to defining the lesser included offense of murder known as voluntary manslaughter. A person commits voluntary manslaughter when that person causes the death of another human being under the circumstances that would otherwise be murder if that person acts solely as the result of sudden violent and irresistible passion resulting from serious provocation sufficient to excite such passion in a reasonable person.

The trial court further charged:

I have prepared a form of verdict. It outlines the counts and also shows an alternative to murder, the lesser included offense of voluntary manslaughter. And I will tell you again that voluntary manslaughter is a lesser included offense of murder so they are mutually exclusive. With regard to the lesser included offense, after consideration of all of the evidence, before you would be authorized to return a verdict of guilty of malice murder or felony murder, you must first determine whether mitigating evidence, if any, would cause the offense to be reduced to voluntary manslaughter.

Kendrick argues that the trial court's failure to inform the jury that voluntary manslaughter is a lesser included offense of felony murder at two points in the final charge is error and is not cured by the fact that the trial court did charge the jury on that point prior to deliberation in its third mention of voluntary manslaughter. We disagree.

This Court does not require the trial courts to follow an exact formula in instructing juries so long as the charge as a whole ensures that the jury will consider whether evidence of provocation and passion might authorize a verdict of voluntary manslaughter. As a whole, the instruction in this case did not prevent the jury from fully considering voluntary manslaughter, and was adequate to inform the jury that before they could convict of malice or felony murder, they must first consider whether there was sufficient evidence of passion or provocation to support a conviction for voluntary manslaughter.

ANALYSIS

Kendrick's conviction for felony murder was affirmed. The court found the evidence sufficient to support the jury's verdict even though there was some disputed testimony that the victim shot first. The court also found that the trial judge's instruction on the lesser offense of voluntary manslaughter was not erroneous, even though the judge did not mention that voluntary manslaughter was a lesser offense of felony murder each time that offense was mentioned.

You should also recognize that the appellate court in this case was clearly *not* endorsing this trial court's instruction; rather, it was simply concluding that the instruction was "good enough" to pass muster to ensure a fair result. Certainly after decisions like this one are handed down, trial courts in the future would need to take care not to "copy" this instruction, but should rather seek to improve upon it, e.g., by specifically mentioning to the jury that voluntary manslaughter is a lesser offense of felony murder each time that offense was mentioned.

Let me add one parenthetical point here. There is no indication in this opinion that Kendrick's defense counsel (at trial) objected to the judge's instructions on the ground subsequently raised in his behalf on appeal. Although the appellate court did not discuss this issue explicitly, part of the reason for the "fairness rule" discussed in this section is that we want to encourage trial counsel to object to any arguable errors *at a time when these mistakes can actually be corrected*. For this reason, appellate courts often hold expressly that appellate counsel cannot raise an issue on appeal based on an error that could have been corrected had trial counsel objected to it, i.e., that objection is deemed to be "waived."

C. DISCUSSING APPELLATE DECISIONS IN CLASS

The instructional methodology of having law students read and analyze appellate cases for class rather than having them simply read and memorize criminal statutes is intended to demonstrate just how important it is in our common law legal system to understand not only what sorts of criminal offenses and defenses exist, but just how these legal constructs apply to a particular set of facts.

Change just one fact, and a sure conviction on a particular charge is no longer possible, e.g., first-degree murder cannot be proved if the accused can show that he or she did not in fact premeditate the killing.

Change just one fact, and a particular defense to a charged crime will no longer work, e.g., self-defense doesn't work when it turns out that it wasn't necessary for the accused to respond to the victim's provocative action with the use of force.

The case method also gives you the opportunity to see and to analyze just how courts actually apply criminal statutes in specific cases and—importantly—to *critique* the courts' analysis. This is a significant point, namely, that while appellate decisions may be binding and precedential in their jurisdiction, their analysis is not necessarily correct.

Your Criminal Law professor will be encouraging you, if not compelling you in Socratic fashion, to second-guess each and every court's analysis and ruling. Did the court get it right? If so, why? If not, why not? You'll want to bear this in mind when you are reading each of the cases in your casebook.

For example, in the *Enimpah* decision, did the trial judge's instructions really set out the prevailing law accurately? If so, is that law sensible? Should the legislature change it and, if so, how? And was the appellate court's analysis of when and how consent could be withdrawn accurate ... and was it sensible? If so, why? If not, why not? You can bet that your Criminal Law professor will be asking questions just like these.

D. CRIMINAL TRIALS ARE DIFFERENT

There is an arguable downside to focusing only, or primarily, upon appellate decisions in your Criminal Law, or any other law school, class. Criminal trials are very, very different from appellate proceedings in criminal cases. It is certainly arguable that by focusing your attention primarily upon the legal issues raised by counsel in an appeal, you are not focusing as much as you could or should on how cases are prepared for trial and actually tried by the prosecution and by the defense.

Many Criminal Law professors share this concern. Some respond to it by using problem-focused or case-file-centered textbooks instead of or in addition to casebooks. Still others will initiate class discussion by focusing on a case in a casebook, but then move to focus class discussion on trial and pretrial-related matters. For example, in the *Kendrick* decision, what could the prosecutor have done to lessen the chance that the defendant could have successfully appealed the jury instructions given to the jury? What could defense counsel have done to raise more of a doubt about the sufficiency of the felony-murder charge?

E. THINKING LIKE LEGISLATORS

When appellate courts are deciding how particular criminal statutes apply to the facts before them, they have no power to change or "improve" those statutes; they can't make them fairer or clearer or more or less comprehensive or inclusive. That's the Legislature's job, not the courts. The Legislature makes the laws. The courts "merely" interpret and apply them. *See* the discussion in Chapter 8.

But your Criminal Law classroom is not an appellate courtroom!

You, of course, *do* have the opportunity, albeit without the actual power, to suggest and to discuss and to debate desirable changes in the law. And you can bet that that is just what is going to happen in your Criminal Law class. In addition to discussing and analyzing the cases, the lawyers' actions and tactics, and the judges' rulings and analysis, you will also most certainly be put into the shoes of the legislators as well.

You will need to focus not just upon how the law is and should be applied, but also on what the law should actually cover and how it should cover it. *Hey, some of you reading these words right now will in fact be legislators!* You'll be making and amending and repealing these criminal statutes. Some day. Maybe not too far off in the future. Who knows? It's far better to think about these matters in your Criminal Law class than to have to pick up these skills in on-the-job training after you're elected, isn't it?

So, after discussing the *Enimpah* decision, for example, you might well be asked, Do you think that the law on when and how consent to sexual intercourse can be withdrawn is sensible and/or clear enough?

And after discussing the *Kendrick* decision, for example, you might well be asked, Do you think that the law on when and how felony murder can be mitigated to voluntary manslaughter is sensible and/or clear enough? What do you think?

F. APPELLATE STANDARDS OF REVIEW

There is another extremely important thing to bear in mind when you are reading and preparing appellate decisions for class, namely that appellate judges are not reviewing the underlying facts of the case *de novo*.

De novo? What does that mean? It means "in the first instance."

The fact-finder in the trial court—the jury or the judge if it is a bench trial (*see* Chapter 5)—"finds the facts" in the first instance. In particular, it is the fact-finder, not an appellate court, that assesses the credibility of witnesses. Who is lying or exaggerating? Who is telling the truth? Appellate judges simply cannot assess that effectively and fairly just by reading a witness's testimony in a transcript ("on a cold record," we sometimes say). And, significantly, we don't expect or allow appellate judges to do that.

It's the judge and the jury who actually see and hear the witness testimony and who actually compare and evaluate conflicting testimony in order to decide what really happened before reaching a verdict in the allegedly criminal episode before the court.

Why is this significant?

Well, it's important because it leads to two very important—and often dispositive—procedural rules that are used by appellate courts in deciding appeals. Those two rules are:

---

1. The facts being considered by the appellate court are considered in the light most favorable to the prosecution, the verdict winner at trial.

and

2. A guilty verdict will be upheld if any reasonable jury could have found the accused guilty on the basis of the facts adduced at trial.

The facts being considered by the appellate court are considered in the light most favorable to the prosecution because the jury found the accused guilty, a verdict in the prosecution's favor. Why is this the rule? Why is this even fair, you might ask?

The answer is that the facts were found by the fact-finder at trial, not by the appellate court. Since the fact-finder was assessing competing and often conflicting factual accounts of what happened, in order to reach a Guilty verdict, it obviously believed the facts presented that favored the prosecution's case. Accordingly, a reviewing court may not reassess the credibility of witnesses, but rather must assume that the jury (or judge in a bench trial) resolved all the evidentiary contradictions in testimony in favor of the Government.

Indeed, that conclusion supports the second important procedural rule as well: A Guilty verdict will be upheld if "any reasonable jury" could have found the accused guilty on the basis of the facts adduced at trial. Sometimes the court talks about a "rational" jury instead of a "reasonable" jury, but the upshot is exactly the same.

Again, it is not the appellate court's job to find the facts. The fact-finder does that. It is the appellate court's task *only* to decide whether *any* reasonable (or rational) jury could have come to the conclusion reached by this jury on the basis of the factual record taken from the trial proceedings.

CASE 28. The meth dealer: Appellate courts review trial court convictions in the light most favorable to the prosecution, asking whether a reasonable jury could have convicted. The Ninth Circuit Court of Appeals did not make its own factual determination of what happened in Pita-Mota's case. That is not what appellate courts do.

Instead, the Ninth Circuit simply asked whether a reasonable jury could have reached the decision that Pita-Mota was guilty of the charged offenses, assessing the evidence introduced at trial in the light most favorable to the prosecution. The court's answer? Yes. The jury's verdict was rational when applying this standard. As a result, Pita-Mota's narcotics convictions were affirmed.

UNITED STATES v. FELIX PITA-MOTA
2012 WL 1407054 (9th Cir. 2012).

The Court: Felix Pita-Mota appeals his criminal conviction for (1) conspiracy to distribute and possess with intent to distribute 500 grams or more of methamphetamine; (2) distribution and possession with intent to distribute 500 grams or more of methamphetamine; (3) use of a firearm in furtherance of a drug transaction; and (4) possession of a firearm by a convicted felon. We affirm.

We hold that sufficient evidence supported the jury verdicts. We engage in a two-step process when considering a defendant's challenge to the sufficiency of the evidence: We first construe the evidence in the light most favorable to the prosecution, and we then determine whether any rational trier of fact could have found the essential elements of the crime beyond a reasonable doubt.

Viewed in the light most favorable to the prosecution, we easily conclude that a rational trier of fact could have found the essential elements of the crime beyond a reasonable doubt. A rational jury could have concluded that Pita-Mota was a participant in the conspiracy and had a role of providing protection for the drug transaction. Pita-Mota offers an alternative story that suggests innocent explanations for this behavior, but nothing required the jury to believe that version of the events.

ANALYSIS

Pita-Mota's convictions were all affirmed because, despite some contrary evidence, a reasonable jury could have found all of the elements of the crime to have existed beyond a reasonable doubt on the evidence introduced at trial.

CASE 29. The crooked car leaser: Appellate courts are not fact-finders. The Texas Criminal Court of Appeals did not make its own factual determination of what happened in Wirth's case. That is, once again, simply not what appellate courts do.

Instead, the Texas court simply asked whether a reasonable jury could have reached the decision that Wirth was guilty of theft, assessing the evidence introduced at trial in the light most favorable to the prosecution. The court's answer? Yes. The jury's verdict was rational when applying this standard. As a result, Wirth's theft conviction was affirmed.

RAYMOND WIRTH v. STATE OF TEXAS
361 S.W.3d 694 (Tex. Crim. Ct. App. 2012).

The Court: Raymond Wirth owned and operated a car-leasing business which acted as an intermediary between car dealerships and customers. In a typical transaction, after being approached by a customer interested in leasing a vehicle, Wirth's business would locate a vehicle, obtain approval of the interested lessee by a financing bank, arrange for the purchase of the vehicle, arrange for transfer of title to the bank, and assign the agreement to the financing bank. When an agreement had been reached, the business's general manager, James Rogers, would issue a sight draft [a "sight draft" is simply a bill payable upon presentation] to the car dealership, to be paid later out of the business's bank account. Rogers testified that Wirth authorized him to issue drafts, but that he was not authorized to issue checks to cover the drafts.

In March of 2005, Wirth closed the business's bank accounts and withdrew the balances. The business ceased operations shortly thereafter, and in its wake, five car dealerships discovered that they possessed worthless drafts with combined face values of over $500,000. These dealerships made repeated attempts to contact Wirth, to no avail, and the business failed to pay any of the outstanding drafts. At trial, the bank's account manager testified that, in the year preceding the business's closing, she and Wirth had frequently spoken about the fact that the business's account did not always contain sufficient funds to honor the business's outstanding drafts.

Wirth was charged by indictment for the offense of theft over $200,000. The jury found the appellant guilty of the lesser-included offense of theft of $20,000 or more but less than $100,000.

A person commits the offense of theft if he unlawfully appropriates property with intent to deprive the owner of property. A claim of theft made in connection with a contract, however, requires proof of more than an intent to deprive the owner of property and subsequent appropriation of the property. In that circumstance, the State must prove that the appropriation was a result of a false pretext, or fraud. Moreover, the evidence must show that the accused intended to deprive the owner of the property at the time the property was taken. In reviewing the sufficiency of the evidence, though, we should look at events occurring before, during and after the commission of the offense and may rely on actions of the defendant which show an understanding and common design to do the prohibited act.

While the evidence in this case is not overwhelming, neither is it so weak as to require an acquittal; it is well settled that the reviewing court must view the evidence in the light most favorable to the verdict. There is no evidence that Wirth directly signed any drafts. The jury was charged on the law of parties, however, and there was sufficient evidence to support a finding that Wirth authorized the transfer of title of automobiles knowing that he would be unable or unwilling to satisfy the issued drafts. Furthermore, there were numerous occurrences of insufficient funds in the year preceding the close of the business, Wirth requested the withdrawal of all funds despite knowing of outstanding drafts, Wirth bounced checks to cover dishonored drafts, and (perhaps most importantly) Wirth authorized the general manager (Rogers) to sign drafts, but not to sign checks to satisfy the drafts.

The evidence in this case is almost entirely circumstantial. Accordingly, the evidence here could merely be symptoms of a previously successful business falling off and scrambling for money from any available source. But we are not the fact finder. The jury inferred from this circumstantial evidence that Wirth authorized Rogers to issue drafts to car dealerships knowing that he would never satisfy them. This was not a determination so outrageous that no rational trier of fact could agree. Our review of the record reveals legally sufficient evidence to support the jury's verdict of guilt.

ANALYSIS

Wirth's conviction for theft was affirmed because there was sufficient, albeit conflicting and circumstantial, evidence for the trial jury to have found that he authorized his general manager, Rogers, to issue drafts to car dealerships knowing that he would never satisfy them.

After reading the *Wirth* and the (bare-bones) *Pita-Mota* decisions and thinking about the procedural rules under discussion above for just a little bit, you may very well have reached an important conclusion, namely that trial court convictions will rarely be reversed on the ground that they are not supported by the evidence.

If this is the conclusion you reached, well, *congratulations ... you're absolutely right!*

The facts are found at the trial court level. The appellate court does not look at these facts de novo, but simply decides if a reasonable (or rational) jury could have found what it found while viewing the evidence in the light most favorable to the prosecution. Using a lens like this with which to view the trial court disposition, appellate courts rarely reverse on the ground that a trial court conviction was not supported by the evidence.

But, that said . . . *sometimes* . . . *just sometimes* . . .

CASE 30. The guy in the car during the robbery: Sometimes a reasonable jury could not have convicted. The Ohio Court of Appeals did not make its own factual determination of what happened in Martin's case. As you saw in the *Pita-Mota* and *Wirth* decisions, that is simply *not* what appellate courts do.

Instead, the Ohio court asked whether a reasonable jury could have reached the decision that Martin was guilty of robbery, looking only to the evidence introduced at trial in the light most favorable to the prosecution. And this time, the court's answer was No. No rational jury could have reached this verdict on this evidence. As a result, Martin's robbery conviction was reversed.

STATE OF OHIO v. BRYNN MARTIN
2012 WL 1139123 (Ohio Ct. App. 4 Dist. 2012).

The Court: Martin argues that insufficient evidence exists to support his conviction for robbery. An appellate court's function when reviewing the sufficiency of the evidence to support a criminal conviction is to examine the evidence admitted at trial to determine whether such evidence, if believed, would convince the average mind of the defendant's guilt beyond a reasonable doubt. The relevant inquiry is whether, after viewing the evidence in a light most favorable to the prosecution, any rational trier of fact could have found the essential elements of the crime proven beyond a reasonable doubt.

This test raises a question of law and does not allow the appellate court to weigh the evidence. A sufficiency of the evidence challenge tests whether the state's case is legally adequate to go to a jury in that it contains prima facie evidence of all of the elements of the charged offense. A conviction that is based on legally insufficient evidence constitutes a denial of due process. Martin specifically argues that the state failed to present evidence from which a rational juror could conclude that he committed all the necessary elements of robbery, including that he "inflicted, attempted to inflict or threatened to inflict physical harm on another." He claims the only direct evidence of his involvement with the crime presented by the state was the testimony of Rhonda Oiler, who testified that Martin told her he drove to the scene, but never went into the house. Because the jury was not instructed on complicity, he claims there was insufficient evidence to convict him of robbery. We agree.

The record reveals that the only connection between Martin and the robbery of Mr. Sowards was the testimony of Special Agents Jenkins and Willis, and that of Oiler. Special Agent Jenkins testified that Martin admitted that he knew Shawn Lawson and that they made "a plan." He also stated that Martin admitted he was the driver for Lawson on the night of Mr. Sowards' murder. Special Agent Willis testified that Martin also admitted that Lawson had approached him about helping and he had known about the plan for a long time. However, there was no testimony presented by the state explaining what "the plan" actually consisted of. Willis also testified that Martin admitted that he was the driver, but he claimed he never actually entered Mr. Sowards' home.

There was also testimony presented by the state that Martin was excluded as the possible source of DNA under Mr. Sowards' fingernails and no other physical evidence connected him to the crime scene.

In summary, the state failed to present any testimony or physical evidence showing that Martin entered Mr. Sowards' home on the date in question and inflicted, attempted to inflict, or threatened to inflict physical harm upon him. Even after viewing the evidence in a light most favorable to the prosecution, we conclude no rational trier of fact could have found beyond a reasonable doubt that Martin committed all the necessary elements of the offense. Thus, the evidence in this case does not support Martin's conviction for robbery as the principal offender.

ANALYSIS

Martin's conviction for robbery as a principal offender was reversed because the Ohio Court of Appeals concluded that no reasonable jury could have found all of the elements of robbery to be present, including that he "inflicted, attempted to inflict or threatened to inflict physical harm on another," on the basis of the factual record before the trial court. There was not even any record evidence introduced showing that he entered the victim's home.

One final, if parenthetical, point here.

If you read the three decisions set out above, *Pita-Mota*, *Wirth*, and *Martin*, and *only* these three decisions, in a law school class, you might well decide that sometimes appellate courts find that the evidence introduced at trial supported the jury's verdict (*Pita-Mota* and *Wirth*) and sometimes they find that it didn't support the jury's verdict (*Martin*). Well, that's certainly true enough.

But what you won't have seen from just looking at those three cases is this: In the overwhelming majority of cases, as previously noted, trial court convictions are rarely reversed on the ground that they are not supported by the evidence.

You see, casebook authors often seek to give you a balanced view, trying to show you that courts sometimes affirm and sometimes reverse, applying the same rules of law to different factual scenarios. I'm a casebook author. I do exactly that. But the point is only this: Don't assume just because you read and discuss one or two cases going one way and another one or two cases going the other way that that numerical ratio reflects the actual distribution of appellate holdings in similar cases handed down all over the country. It doesn't.

CHAPTER 12

Taking Criminal Law Exams for Fun and Profit

A. WHAT MATERIALS SHOULD YOU USE TO PREPARE FOR A CRIMINAL LAW EXAM?

YOUR NOTES

The absolute best resource you have available to prepare to take an exam in Criminal Law is your own notes. If you've been an accurate and regular note-taker, your notes should reflect each and every one of the important substantive points that your professor has been trying to teach you during the course.

Moreover, as you continue to review, going over (and over and over) your own notes, that process of periodic review itself should help you to burn those points into your memory.

There's another thing to bear in mind. You will probably also prepare for your exam by consulting some secondary sources, like treatises or commercial outlines or study aids. Well, the author of each and every one of those secondary sources—usually another law professor, not your teacher—is not the person who will be grading your exam! Obviously. But the point is that if *your* professor has made a somewhat different point than the point that you have read in a secondary source, use your teacher's approach on the exam, not the approach of the secondary source. Remember, it's your teacher who is grading your exam!

Of course, if your notes make a point significantly different from the point that you find being made in secondary sources, you may also want to check on the accuracy of your note-taking. How can you do that? Easy. Ask your professor.

Or, if he or she is not available (or if you've been asking way too many questions and don't want to appear to be a nuisance), then maybe this is a good time to consult other students in your class or members of your study group, if you have one. Do they have the very same point in their notes that you have in yours? It's possible that maybe, just maybe, your notes were a "little off" that day. Hey, it happens!

OUTLINES

Almost everyone who has taken a law school course will tell you this: Synthesizing your own notes and the additional information you have obtained from secondary sources into a comprehensive but cogent outline is probably the most useful tool you have to prepare for an exam. This is true for two different reasons.

First, once you have made your outline, this can and *should* be your primary exam preparation reference source. All the basic substantive points of law that you have discussed during the course of the semester should be right there, right in front of you, for easy reference.

But, second, and maybe even more important, *the process* of making your outline, distilling the important points to include in it from your notes and from any other sources of information that you are consulting, is extremely useful in and of itself.

Putting together an outline forces you to figure out and to focus your attention upon the most important points in what may be a virtual mountain of factual and analytical (and, frankly, sometimes extraneous) material. It is often true that when law students are in a study group and one member of that group is charged with the task of making an outline for the rest of the group for a particular class, that that study group member knows the material better for that class and, often, does better or the best on the exam. No surprise, right?

CASEBOOKS

In some law school courses, your course casebook should be an important part of your exam preparation. But, significantly, that is usually *not* the case for a course in Criminal Law.

Why is that?

The answer is that a casebook is typically only useful for exam preparation if the decisions included in the book are themselves important to remember. That's invariably the case, for example, in a course in Constitutional Law or Criminal Procedure. In those courses, the decisions included in the casebook are often binding Supreme Court precedents. They stand for something in and of themselves. Even the names of the cases may be shorthand for a legal point, e.g., *Miranda* warnings. These dispositive holdings bind the lower courts, and the Supreme Court's analysis is, for that reason, extremely important, influential, and precedential.

But that is not the case, in contrast, in a course like Criminal Law. In Criminal Law, decisions are included in a casebook *only* for the purpose of giving you *an example* of how appellate courts deal with specific Criminal

Law—usually statutory—issues. The statutes the included cases deal with are usually only the statutes that are in force in that particular jurisdiction. And these decisions themselves are *not* precedential except in the specific jurisdiction in which that court sits.

So, for example, a Nebraska Court of Appeals decision dealing with a conspiracy law issue may be a very good vehicle for discussing one or more of the elements of the offense of conspiracy in your class, or the difference between unilateral versus bilateral conspiracy statutes, or the various defenses to conspiracy, or how courts approach and apply conspiracy statutes. But—*sorry Cornhuskers!*—the decision itself is simply no big deal! It is not precedential outside of Nebraska and, even then, only if it has not been overruled by a higher court or the statute under discussion amended or repealed by the Nebraska legislature.

In short, the likely reason that that decision was included in your casebook was simply as a vehicle to prompt discussion of some particular aspect or a number of aspects of conspiracy law, not because the decision was important in and of itself. Except maybe in Nebraska.

There is one caveat, however. Your "casebook" will likely contain something other than cases, namely discussion in notes prior and subsequent to excerpts from the decisions you have read and discussed in class. Now *that* material—unlike the decisions themselves—may be very useful to you for purposes of exam preparation. Those textual comments may well be just the sort of material from which you will want to cull some substantive gems to put in your outline.

TOPIC LISTS

I always recommend to my Criminal Law students that they create for themselves one additional document to use in the course of their exam preparation: A short, *very short*, topic list.

A topic list is particularly useful for open-book exams that contain one or more issue-spotting questions, as I will discuss in just a moment. But it's also a useful tool for any other kind of Criminal Law exam.

What do I mean by a topic list? Well, I mean just what the phrase implies: A very brief—one page is plenty—list of the topics that you have covered in your specific Criminal Law course.

Why would you need that? How is it useful? The answer is that a list like that, whether you have it with you because the exam is open book or whether you have been consulting it prior to the exam because the exam is closed book, can be very useful simply to help you remember precisely what topics might be included in any specific Criminal Law exam question.

Look, law school exams are stressful. Very stressful. You are under a lot of pressure. Time is short. Often, you are not thinking as clearly as you would be

---

Example of a Criminal Law Topic List

Justifications for punishment	Involuntary manslaughter
Sexual offenses	Causation
Force vs. lack of consent	Attempt
Actus reus	Substantial step vs. proximity tests
Involuntary act	Abandonment defense
Omissions	Impossibility
Mens rea	Conspiracy
Intoxication or drugged condition	Unilateral vs. bilateral
Strict liability	Overt act
Vicarious culpability	Complicity
Corporate responsibility	Self-defense
Mistake of fact	Deadly force
Mistake of law	Retreat
First-degree murder	Defense of others
Premeditation and deliberation	Defense of property
Reckless murder	Defense of habitation
Malice	Stand Your Ground laws
Voluntary manslaughter:	Insanity
Provocation defense	Guilty but mentally ill
Imperfect defenses	Diminished capacity

---

in a less pressurized situation. The point is that in a stressful environment like that, you might simply miss the fact that, in a particular exam question, a number of issues are being raised, not just one or two. The topic list helps you to remember everything that has been covered so that you aren't as likely to miss something.

For example, take conspiracy law again. An exam question might clearly focus on whether or not a conspiracy existed. And you think to yourself right away: Okay, so I have to talk about whether this is a unilateral or bilateral jurisdiction, whether a conspiratorial intent and agreement existed, and whether or not there was an overt act committed by one of the conspirators (all common elements of conspiracy). But . . . you might forget—in the heat of the exam battle—that there are affirmative defenses to the crime of conspiracy, too. And one or more of those defenses might well be tenable in the factual circumstances you have been presented, e.g., withdrawal or abandonment.

If you have a topic list with you (open-book exam) or in your head (closed-book exam prep), you may well "scroll through" that list, and when you quickly view or recall the phrase, "Abandonment Defense," you may have one of those *aha* moments when you remember that—abandonment—is an issue that you should discuss in your exam answer.

That's all there is to it. A topic list is not another outline or even a mini-outline. It is simply a list of the topics—one word or a simple phrase is all you need—that you covered in your particular Criminal Law class that you can use as a reminder to jog your memory.

Here's an example of a Topic List. But . . . warning . . . don't just copy this one to use yourself. Remember, every Criminal Law class is different in precisely what is and what is not covered. And you should also remember that, just as with outlines, the making of the list is as or more important than merely having the list with you.

You should also make sure your topic list includes the topics that were listed in your course syllabus (if they were listed there), the topics included in your notes, and the topics listed in the sections of the casebook that you were assigned to read.

See how short this sample Topic List is? That's all you need. Again, this is not intended to be just another, shorter outline. It's simply intended to jog your memory.

TREATISES

There are a number of excellent treatises (sometimes called "hornbooks") on Criminal Law that you can find in your law library's collection. Some of them are more concise than others; some of them are more or less analytical than others. Because they are so different, if you consult one of them and you don't find it particularly helpful, don't assume as a result that *all* of the Criminal Law treatises will be like that for you. They are all different—in length, tone, format, etc. Take a look at another one if the first one doesn't suit you for some reason. You may find that another one contains more of the kind of guidance that you were looking for.

In my view, the real value of these treatises is *not* to serve as regular, supplementary reading throughout the time you are taking your Criminal Law course. Instead, the most effective use of a Criminal Law treatise is to help you out in the specific instances when you are confused about particular subject areas.

Take the subject of the abandonment or withdrawal defense in conspiracy law as an example. Perhaps your professor's discussion of this topic was confusing, at least to you. Or maybe he or she simply didn't discuss that issue sufficiently, or even at all, leaving you to pick up the points you needed to learn from your reading in the casebook. Or maybe you just don't remember the classroom discussion, and your notes are unhelpful or confusing. Hey, this may be precisely the moment to take a look at a Criminal Law treatise.

Just lean back in your chair and read the section that deals with this specific conspiracy law defense that has confused you. Hopefully, the treatise author's discussion will dispel or at least alleviate your confusion. If so, then that treatise has become an extremely valuable resource for you.

COMMERCIAL OUTLINES AND STUDY AIDS

Law professors take very different positions on the question of when—if ever—their students should use commercial outlines or study aids, either in preparing for class or in preparing to take a Criminal Law examination.

Some professors take the position that using such resources is a very bad idea because when you have access to such materials, the temptation may be for you not to actually read the cases and do the analysis yourself, but to rely instead on someone else's having done that work, the study aid author.

Frankly, if that is the way you intend to use a commercial outline or study aid, that really is a mistake; it's a disservice to yourself. The point of reading cases in a Criminal Law course is *not* simply so that you can find out "what the rule is." Rather, the primary objective of assigning you to review and to prepare cases for class is for you to learn *how to do the analysis* to figure out what the rule is, what it should be, and what it is likely to be or should be in the next case. It's the analysis—the process—that's key, not simply the holding. And the holding—the rule of law—is what some commercial outlines and some study aids tend to focus upon.

That said, I think that the appropriate use of commercial outlines and study aids can be quite helpful. Okay, in the interest of full disclosure, maybe I take that position in some small part because I am the author or co-author of some widely used Criminal Law study aids, including *Inside Criminal Law: What Matters and Why* (Aspen Publishers/Wolters Kluwer Law & Business) (Second Edition, 2011). But it seems to me that any tool that can help you understand the material you are studying better than you would otherwise is a useful resource. Maybe study aids should be used like alcohol, i.e., only in moderation!

STUDY GROUPS

Many law students form study groups to discuss class assignments, to share notes and questions, to empathize with and support one another, and to jointly prepare for exams. This is particularly true in the first year of law school, and Criminal Law is often a first-year course.

In my view, study groups can be a very useful resource, *inter alia*, for exam preparation. Members of the group can discuss the applicable rules of law and work on "taking" sample exam questions together and discussing the best answers and strategies for answering those questions. But members of a study group need to take care not to become reliant on other members of the group. While it may be more efficient to parcel out outlining responsibilities, for example, do remember that you lose the opportunity to focus more intensely on and become more familiar with the course subject matter if you don't prepare *your own* outline. Similarly, in preparing for an exam, while it may be more efficient to parcel out exam preparation responsibilities to other members of the group, you do lose the opportunity to focus more intensely on and become more familiar with the course subject matter your-self if you become overly reliant on *someone else's* work and preparation.

One other point. If you are in a study group, you must take care not to fall prey to one of the perils of group thinking; namely, letting other people convince you that they are correct and that you are not. You're discussing a sample exam question, for example, and the other three members of your group talk you out of the answer you think is correct and convince you that their answer is correct instead. Hey, you may have been right! Or, you know what? Law is not like math. There rarely is only one possible answer. You all may have been right, even though you argued for different answers! The point is only this: You still need to do your own work, do your own analysis, and come to your own conclusions, even if you are working in a group.

OLD EXAMS

Where they are available, one of the best exam preparation resources you can use is old examinations previously given by the specific professor who has taught your course. Not only are these old questions obviously useful for purposes of self-examination, especially in the days just prior to the exam administration, in order to make sure that you "know your stuff," but they may well be *more* useful for another reason.

If you're in Law School right now, remember when you took the LSAT (I'm sure you do) and you probably took an LSAT prep course or used an LSAT prep book, a DVD, or an on-line program to prepare for the test? The value of that course or that preparation was mostly not to "tell you the answers," was it? No, it wasn't. The value of that preparation was to acquaint you with *the type of questions* being asked and the way in which you should approach and answer them.

It's the same with Criminal Law examinations that your professor has used in the past. Looking at those questions and attempting to answer them can give you a good sense of the way in which *your specific professor* examines this subject, the types of issues he or she tends to question about, and hopefully, if he or she is willing to answer questions about these old exam questions, what your professor is looking for in terms of answers.

Law professors are just like everyone else. We tend to repeat our patterns of behavior. My new Criminal Law exams tend to look a lot like my old Criminal Law exams. Not in terms of the factual circumstances presented and the specific questions asked, to be sure. But they do look alike in terms of the *types* of questions I ask, the way I ask them, and the kinds of responses I am looking for. Just like the LSAT. And it's also not hard when you take a look at a few of my old Criminal Law exams to predict some of the subject areas that are likely to be examined. I'm pretty sure that, in decades of teaching this course, I have *never* given a final exam in Criminal Law where some poor soul or other didn't die. Don't ignore homicide law in your preparation!

ONE FINAL PARENTHETICAL POINT

This isn't a point about *the materials* you should use in exam prep, but rather about how you should go about preparing. As previously mentioned (and you won't be surprised when I say this), law school exams are stressful. Very, very, very stressful. There is a lot riding on your performance. Particularly in the first year. That's a shame, of course. And it's probably wrong and unnecessary. But it's nonetheless true. It's a fact.

My point here is that you need to realize this and to prepare for it. How? Well, you need to focus not just on the substantive material to be learned for the exam, but also on *how and when and where* you're going to go about learning it.

You need, for example, to set a schedule for yourself that keeps you working and learning right up to the day of the exam. You don't want, in contrast, to "peak" too soon, to be done with your studying (and your short-term memory cramming) 2 or 3 days too early. That's a mistake.

You also need to think about *where* you want to do your studying. Can you work at home? Is it quiet there? Or is it too quiet and too subject to temptation? Is your Xbox or bed just sitting there in your apartment, 5 feet away from your desk, calling your name? If you work better away from home, is your school's law library the best place? Do you have too many friends who are also studying there who keep interrupting you? Are there other libraries or quiet spots on campus that your law school friends don't know about? Check it out!

Are you prone to pulling all-nighters and then thinking and acting like a zombie the next day? Do you really work best like that? Or does it just happen? If I could only offer you one piece of tactical advice for the pre-exam period, it would be this: Get enough sleep! Really.

Look, I can't tell you how *you* can or should best get ready for a Criminal Law exam. You've got to do it your own way. People are different. But what I am telling you is this: Think about it. Have a plan. Have a strategy. And don't psych yourself out. Maybe "reward" yourself with little rewards for keeping to your study schedule . . . with a movie, or a long bath, or something you like to eat but usually don't permit yourself. Basically, pamper yourself a little bit. This is the moment.

B. OPEN-BOOK VS. CLOSED-BOOK EXAMS

The primary difference between taking an open-book rather than a closed-book Criminal Law exam should essentially be one of organization, not preparation. If you are taking an open-book Criminal Law exam, you want to have all of the materials that you are taking into the exam room with you well and clearly organized.

Why do I say that? Well, there are some people who argue that there really should be no significant difference in preparation for an open-book or a closed-book exam. Their rationale is usually that there is rarely much time to thumb through your casebook or notes or a commercial outline (if that is permitted as part of the open-book protocol for your exam). So in the end, there is no need to prepare any differently because you won't really use the materials you have brought in with you effectively, or at all, given the tight time constraints. And, some argue further, if you know that you can take materials with you into the exam room, you might respond to that advantage by slacking off, by failing to do the type of reading and rereading and thinking that you would do if you knew you would not have those materials available. "Hey, why go over them now? I'll have them with me in the exam room."

I disagree.

I think that the primary value to you of taking an open-book exam is the opportunity it gives you to *refresh your memory* from the materials you have taken in with you. In my view, I don't see test-takers randomly thumbing through their casebooks or notes, wildly searching for answers. That's just not going to work, and you know it.

Instead, I see test-takers glancing quickly and efficiently at well-organized outlines, notes, or topic lists. By "well organized," what I mean is that you have worked with the materials you've brought into the room enough times and you've set them up in such a way that you know exactly where everything is. As a result, if you want to quickly check on the elements of conspiracy law—just for a second, to make sure you got it right in your answer—you know exactly where to look in your outline. And depending on how compulsive (or well prepared) you really are, maybe your outline is keyed to your notes and/or your casebook if you need a more detailed review so you can get to the proper section quickly, without any fuss or panic.

Moreover, as previously discussed, open-book, issue-spotting exams are the setting where topic lists are most useful. After you've read the question and thought about (and memorized briefly) the points you need to make to respond effectively, then, *only then*, glance at the topics list. Quickly scan all of the topics listed. Was there something else in that question you just read that you needed to address? *Oh yeah! Wait a minute!* The guy in the problem was drinking a beer, wasn't he? You need to address the issue of a possible intoxication defense, don't you?

That's the sort of opportunity you have in an open-book exam where you have a topics list sitting there on the table in front of you. It's really helpful. Or, at least, it can be.

C. ISSUE-SPOTTING QUESTIONS

One of the most common and notorious forms of law school exam questions, particularly in Criminal Law courses, is the so-called "issue-spotter." An issue-spotting question in Criminal Law is one where the student is presented with a factual scenario and then asked what tenable defenses an accused person may have and/or what the prosecution's chances of success are in bringing certain criminal charges against him or her.

The test-taker's challenge is not only to demonstrate a good grasp of the substantive Criminal Law principles raised in the question, but also and initially to identify all of the possible, relevant issues contained in the question. This is not an easy task! But it probably could go without saying, if you don't identify a significant issue contained in the factual recitation, then obviously, you can't discuss it and your grade will suffer (just as your client will suffer if you miss important issues as an attorney).

So . . . much of the "art" of taking issue-spotting exams is not simply remembering and reciting the law, but learning how to find the significant issues in any given set of facts and applying the law to those issues and facts.

Let's take a look at an example of an issue-spotting question. This is one that I used on a Fall 2011 Criminal Law exam. There's a lot going on in the question, as you will see. My students had 75 minutes to answer the four subquestions posed to them at the end of this question. Issue-spotting questions like these are often taken, just as this one was, from recent appellate court decisions. This particular one was taken from two different decisions in two different states, with the facts mashed together a bit in order to create some additional, unique issues.

Sometimes, questions like these are not taken from actual decisions, however, but instead are simply factual hypotheticals made up by your professor who is trying to jam a number of different issues in a number of different subject areas into one question. Often these hypothetical questions are said to take place in hypothetical jurisdictions, not real states, e.g., the State of Euphoria or Dyslexia or Ecstasy.

The reason why Criminal Law professors do this is that they do not want you to apply *only* the law of a single state to the facts presented. Nor do you usually need to know the Criminal Law of a particular state. Rather, they want you to discuss the various majority and minority positions that you have discussed in class or read about with respect to the areas of the law covered on the exam. Additionally, some professors simply ask you to apply the provisions of the Model Penal Code to the facts you have been given to analyze. In that case, you do not need to worry about majority and minority positions, just the MPC position.

Now, you can't really *answer* this issue-spotting question example because you haven't finished your Criminal Law course! You don't know all the legal principles . . . *yet*. But . . . there are some nonsubstantive things I can still point out to you taken from this example question that may well be of use to you when you do begin to prepare for an examination like this later on.

The comments in the margins refer to the places in the example question where a number appears in superscript in square brackets.

EXAMPLE OF A CRIMINAL LAW ISSUE-SPOTTING EXAM QUESTION

1. As you are reading this information quickly, you don't want to miss the fact that he had drunk six beers. Even if the rest of the scenario did not further indicate the possibility of inebriation, this beer-drinking fact tips you off that you need to discuss a potential intoxication defense. You always need to think carefully about what these facts reveal to you about possible issues.

On July 1, 2005, after spending several hours in a bar in Manhattan, at which he consumed at least six beers,[1] Martin Heidgen attended a friend's party in Nassau County. He arrived at the party between 11 P.M. and midnight. At the party, Heidgen was seen consuming several alcoholic drinks. Two of his friends who were at the party described Heidgen as intoxicated or "buzzed." However, neither one observed him stumbling or staggering while he was dancing, nor was he observed to be slurring his words. Heidgen remained at the party for 1½ to 2 hours before leaving in his pickup truck.

Shortly before 2:00 A.M. on July 2, 2005, Elizabeth Serwin was driving southbound in the center southbound lane of the Meadowbrook State Parkway, when she saw headlights of an oncoming vehicle driving toward her, also in the center lane; it was in the distance, a "few football fields away." She immediately veered into the right lane and eventually to the shoulder of the road to her right. She honked her horn three times as an oncoming pickup truck, which was later determined to have been operated by Heidgen, passed her. As she looked over her shoulder watching the pickup truck travel northbound in the southbound lanes, she observed two other vehicles pulled over on the shoulder of the road. During the time that Serwin saw the pickup truck, it did not swerve or reduce its speed, which she approximated to be 70 to 75 miles per hour as it passed her.[2]

2. The preceding and the subsequent paragraphs are both loaded with factual accounts of observations of Heidgen's behavior, some of which are simply cumulative and some of them— here's the point!—*may be totally irrelevant* to the questions being asked at the end. It is often the case that you will be given some extraneous factual information in an issue-spotting question. Part of the lawyer's skill is learning to separate important facts from a host of unimportant or simply less important material.

Joseph Caruso, also driving south on the Meadowbrook State Parkway, testified that he first saw the pickup truck approximately 1 mile north of the location where Serwin veered out of the path of the pickup truck. Caruso saw the headlights of the pickup truck about a quarter of a mile away, directly in his path of travel. Caruso attempted to move to the left southbound lane, but the pickup truck tracked him and also moved toward the left lane, causing Caruso to steer back to the center lane to avoid a collision with the northbound pickup truck. As the pickup truck was almost upon Caruso's vehicle, Caruso moved into the right southbound lane, just as the pickup truck passed his vehicle. Once the pickup truck passed, Caruso observed the tail lights of the pickup truck in his rear view mirror and noted that the brake lights never illuminated during the time he had them in view. Caruso also noticed that the pickup truck did not veer away or slow down as it headed toward him. He estimated that the pickup truck was traveling at a rate of speed between 70 and 80 miles per hour.

At the same time that Heidgen was driving the wrong way (north) in the southbound lanes of the Meadowbrook State Parkway, a limousine was proceeding south in the left south-bound lane. The limousine, driven by Stanley Rabinowitz, was carrying a family, consisting of Jennifer Flynn and Neil Flynn, their two daughters, seven-year-old Katie Flynn and five-year-old Grace Flynn, and Jennifer's parents, Christopher Tangney and Denise Tangney, back home from the wedding of the Tangneys' youngest daughter.

Upon observing the pickup truck as it was heading directly toward the limousine, Rabinowitz attempted to veer into the center lane to avoid it. However, there was another south-bound vehicle traveling in the center lane alongside the limousine. The driver of that vehicle, Jeri Montgomery, did not notice that Rabinowitz was trying to move over into her lane or that he was frantically waving at her to move over because she was talking on her cell phone and not paying attention to what was going on around her.[3] At the very last second, Montgomery did finally see Rabinowitz's frantic gestures and, in response, she "rather abruptly" swerved into the right lane to let him in. But when she swerved right, she struck the left rear bumper of the car in the right lane ahead of her, causing it to careen out of control, flip over, and come to rest upside down, killing the driver, Chance Wilcox, who had not been wearing a seatbelt.[4]

Meanwhile, the pickup truck collided head-on with the limousine, having tracked the limousine's movement from lane to lane. This collision crushed and killed Rabinowitz, decapitated Katie Flynn, and caused severe injuries to each of the five remaining passengers in the limousine.

Heidgen was arrested at the scene, and told the police that from the time he had moved to New York from Arkansas the previous October, "everything was going wrong" and "nothing he did was ever enough." Heidgen recounted to the police that he had argued with his ex-girlfriend over the phone, had financial problems, had recently lost his grandmother

3. As you are reading these facts, it is important for you not to simply focus on one actor alone. Heidgen starts out, clearly, as the "bad guy," but—*note!*—at this point, you become aware that Montgomery is also making mistakes. You want to focus on her actions as well and her potential culpability.

4. Don't miss this. Wilcox wasn't wearing a seatbelt. Is that against the law in this jurisdiction? Even if it was illegal, does that make a difference when someone else's—*criminal?*—actions resulted in Wilcox's death? You'll need to deal with this question.

5. Don't miss this emotional material from Heidgen. Could any of this help to make out a tenable defense? You would need to deal with this, too.

6. Your professor may think that he or she is funny and puts (allegedly) funny material into the exam question. I do this all the time. Can't help myself. And, as here, I often make myself the DA or PD in my own exams and have someone unexpected "play" my part. (I don't really look much like Lindsay Lohan.) You are allowed to smile or chuckle at these sorts of attempts at humor, but the important point is to not get distracted by them. Just laugh or shake your head and then . . . *move on!* Don't think that you have to take the time to try and make a joke back in your answer. There is no need, and you don't have that kind of time.

7. "Chances of success." Don't miss that. Your professor is not only asking you to assess all of the issues from the prosecution's point of view, but *also* to assess the merits of those issues. What that tells you is that you also have to look at the defense reaction to each of the issues. If there is a good defense argument against prosecution for a particular charge, the chances of success are slim.

8. *Important!* Don't miss the fact that there are four, distinct sub-questions here. You need to make sure that you answer *each and every one of them.*

9. "*Any* homicide charges," *note!* "*Any!*" Don't miss that part of the question. By asking you about *any* possible homicide charge, your professor is telling you that you need to discuss *all* possible homicide charges . . . in order to rule each and every one of them in or out.

with whom he had been close, and was very upset, depressed, and in a "self-destructive mode."[5]

You are an Assistant District Attorney in Nassau County, New York, where these events all took place, having moved to New York State after law school. The District Attorney, John Burkoff (played by Lindsay Lohan),[6] has asked you to evaluate the chances of success[7] of each[8] of the following: (1) Any homicide charges[9] that could tenably be filed against Heidgen for the deaths of Stanley Rabinowitz and Katie Flynn; (2) any homicide charges that could tenably be filed against Montgomery for the death of Chance Wilcox; (3) attempted murder charges to be filed against Heidgen for the injuries to the five surviving passengers in the limousine; and (4) conspiracy charges to be filed against Montgomery for conspiring with Rabinowitz to commit reckless driving by swerving precipitously into the right lane. What is your response to Burkoff/Lohan?

Cf. People v. Heidgen, 930 N.Y.S.2d 199 (App. Div. 2 Dept. 2011); *Montgomery v. State*, 346 S.W.3d 747 (Tex. Ct. App.–Houston 2011).

Answering This Criminal Law Issue-Spotting Exam Question Example

Once again, I realize that you aren't likely—*yet*—in a position where you can possibly answer the legal questions raised in the issue-spotting question example set out above. But . . . I can still give you an example of how—*once you learn the law*—you should approach answering at least one (significant) part of this question.

Let's take the issue of intoxication, for example, an issue that I mentioned in Comment [1] above that should "jump out at you." The issue is raised in this question about how Heidgen's likely intoxication affects his potential culpability for any or all of the potential homicide offenses for which he might be charged. Let's look at the issue of how it might affect his potential culpability for the crime of first-degree murder.

What's the law on intoxication? Your Criminal Law professor will give you much more detail and nuance on this subject, but basically the law is this:

1. Intoxication (or drugged condition) is a valid defense in most (but not all) jurisdictions if the crime charged is a "specific intent" crime, but it is not a valid defense if the crime charged is a "general intent" or strict liability offense.
2. A "general intent" crime is one where the prosecution only needs to prove the accused's intent to commit the act that caused the harm at issue (here, various homicide offenses), while a "specific intent" crime is one where the prosecution must prove an additional intent beyond the commission of the act that caused the harm at issue.
3. Where an intoxication (or drugged condition) defense is permitted, the accused person's intoxication must be so extreme that he or she could not possess the criminal intent required for the commission of that offense.

If these points relating to the law of intoxication are confusing to you now, hopefully they will not be after you have studied the subject of mens rea in your Criminal Law class. *See* discussion in Chapter 10. But for now, simply taking these statements of the law relating to intoxication as a given, let me give you a couple of examples of you how you might apply that law to the facts in writing that part of an answer to the issue-spotting exam question set out above.

ADDRESSING THE INTOXICATION ISSUE—EXAMPLE 1: STRONGER

An accused person's intoxication or drugged condition can be a defense to a crime in most jurisdictions if the charged offense is a specific intent offense. In some jurisdictions, however, intoxication is never a good defense.[1] If New York is a majority jurisdiction in this regard, then if Heidgen was so extremely intoxicated that he could not possess the required mens rea, he could have a good defense to a homicide charge containing a specific intent element. If New York does not permit an intoxication defense, then obviously Heidgen can't make it in this case.[2]

A specific intent crime is one where the prosecution must prove an additional intent beyond the commission of the act that caused the harm at issue.[3] First-degree murder is typically considered to be a specific intent crime because in order to establish that offense, the prosecutor must prove not only that the accused intended to commit a killing act that resulted in the death of a victim, but also that the accused actually premeditated and deliberated that killing.[4] So if New York is a majority jurisdiction, then Heidgen can use this defense to a first-degree murder charge.[5]

But Heidgen will only be successful with this defense if he can show that he was so extremely intoxicated that he could not possess the mens rea required for this crime—premeditation and deliberation, the specific intent to kill his victims.[6] Heidgen drank six beers and several more alcoholic drinks over a period of a few hours, and he was described as "buzzed" by some friends. But he also danced without falling, stumbling, or staggering, and he wasn't slurring his words. He was also able to get in his truck and had the motor control to drive on the parkway. On these facts, I don't think it is likely that a jury will conclude that Heidgen was so intoxicated that he could not have possessed the specific intent to kill his victims. As a result, intoxication will not be a good defense for him to a charge of first-degree murder. On the other hand, if the jury does conclude that he was too intoxicated to possess that intent, intoxication would be a good defense for him to that charge.[7]

1. Note that this answer starts with a statement of the applicable rule of law.

2. The general rule of law is then focused upon the specific jurisdiction at issue in this question. If you don't know whether the jurisdiction at issue follows a majority or minority approach (and you usually don't), you need to answer the question either way.

3. Now the answer focuses on the test to determine if a crime is "specific intent."

4. This legal test is applied to one of the possible homicide crimes that might be charged.

5. Now the focus shifts back to the specific jurisdiction at issue in this question.

6. An intoxication defense doesn't work unless the accused was extremely intoxicated, so the answer shifts to focusing on these facts with that test in mind.

7. This is important. This answer reaches a likely conclusion, but also explains what the outcome will be if the jury reaches a contrary decision on the facts. No one expects you to know for sure how a jury will find facts, but you need to make a prediction (e.g., not sufficiently intoxicated to make out a good defense) . . . and also explain what will happen if your prediction is wrong.

ADDRESSING THE INTOXICATION
ISSUE—EXAMPLE 2: WEAKER

Heidgen can try to make an intoxication defense to first-degree murder because that's a specific intent crime.[8] But he probably wasn't drunk enough to do that successfully.[9] He was dancing. He didn't stumble or stagger. He didn't slur his words. He could drive. He just wasn't drunk enough to be able to prove that he couldn't actually intend to kill somebody.[10] So Heidgen cannot make an intoxication defense to first-degree murder successfully.[11, 12]

D. ESSAY QUESTIONS

Some Criminal Law professors like to give you one or more essay questions on their exams. These are not issue-spotting questions, but rather questions that, usually although not invariably, ask you to discuss some of the doctrinal underpinnings of particular Criminal Law subjects.

There are a host of different types of essay questions that you might be asked. It's hard to generalize. Here are a couple of essay-type questions that I have used in the last 2 years:

8. *Wait!* You need the preliminaries here first: What's the relevant rule of law? How and when does it apply? Does it apply in New York? What's a "specific intent crime"? Precisely why is first-degree murder one of those? Those are all important predicates to be raised and discussed before simply reaching a conclusion.

9. *Wait!* Before reaching a conclusion like this, what is the test you are applying here? (Heidgen had to show that he was so extremely intoxicated that he couldn't possess the mens rea required for this crime.) Don't imply it, say it!

10. Good facts here. In fact, not much different from the stronger answer. But . . . there is no context. What test were these facts being measured against?

11. You can predict what a jury will do with these facts, but you can never be sure. *See* Comment [7] above, referring to the text in the stronger answer. The better answer reaches a conclusion about how the law will apply to a given set of facts, often simply a prediction, but it also explains what will happen if that prediction is wrong and the fact-finder finds the facts differently.

12. Don't make the mistake of concluding from these examples that the longer answer is always better. That's just not true. The longer answer often *is* better, but only if it contains a fuller and more complete analysis. Short, cogent answers can be excellent, too, as long as they hit all the points that should be covered. This short answer missed some of those points. Example 2 is not a terrible answer, by the way. It's not terrible at all in the context of responding to a complicated issue-spotting question with very limited time to write an answer. It's simply weaker than Example 1.

EXAMPLE 1 OF A CRIMINAL LAW ESSAY EXAM QUESTION

Consider the following observation made by then-Professor, now Ohio Court of Appeals Judge, Melody Stewart:

> "To many people, the debate on whether a legally enforced general duty to aid should exist is unfortunate. Ideally, rendering some minimal assistance to another in peril should be a morally natural and automatic response. When select individuals are not compelled, for whatever reason, to respond in this fashion, a groundswell of emotions arise. For some, having a law that would punish the failure to act is the solution to such amoral apathy. However, making such inaction criminal as a result of emotional reactions only serves the purpose of making the emotional reactors feel better; it does not effectively encourage or bring about any significant positive change in how individuals will respond to others in peril. In some instances, the laws may even have a chilling effect on altruistic behavior.
>
> "The application by courts of the no-duty doctrine and its common law and statutory exceptions has evolved in a way that adequately analyzes and, more often than not, correctly determines under what circumstances someone should be held criminally responsible or civilly liable for failing to act on behalf of another. Contrary to some beliefs, the law in this area is not static. Not only have courts analyzed and applied the rule and its exceptions in keeping with the times, courts in several jurisdictions have collaterally used instances of assistance and the lack thereof to benefit some individuals and burden others."

Melody J. Stewart, "How Making the Failure to Assist Illegal Fails to Assist: An Observation of Expanding Criminal Omission Liability," 25 Am. J. Crim. L. 385, 434 (1998).

Do you agree with Judge Stewart? Making specific reference to matters discussed in this class, please explain why or why not.

EXAMPLE 2 OF A CRIMINAL LAW ESSAY EXAM QUESTION

You are a Pennsylvania legislator. (*Congratulations!*) A colleague of yours has told you that she is considering introducing a bill to criminalize the possession or use of "novelty" cigarette lighters, lighters that are designed to look like cartoon characters, toys, or guns or that play musical notes or have flashing lights. Her belief is that these novelty items are attractive to children who play with them and then burn themselves. She wants to make such an offense a misdemeanor, punishable by a mandatory minimum of 3 days in jail for a first offense, 30 days in jail for a second offense, and 1 year for a third or subsequent offense.

(1) Considering expressly the rationales for criminal punishment discussed in this course, do you think that this is a good and sensible piece of legislation? Explain why or why not.

(2) Whatever your views of the merits (or lack thereof) of this proposed legislation, if it is likely to be enacted, what *mens rea*, if any, do you think should be included as an element of this crime? Explain your choice.

Suppose further that this proposed legislation would add an *additional* mandatory 60-day imprisonment penalty if the novelty cigarette lighter possessed or used is a "torch lighter," a lighter that has a flame that exceeds 4 ½ inches in length.

(3) Should a sentencing judge add this additional penalty to the ordinary sentence she would impose if she decides by a preponderance of evidence in a particular case that the novelty lighter flame possessed by the defendant was 5 inches in length?

(4) Describe what affirmative defenses, if any, you think would be appropriate to add to this legislation. Explain your position.

TIPS FOR ANSWERING ESSAY QUESTIONS

For me, the key to a good answer to an essay question is assessing whether the test-taker has done both of two things: (1) Understood exactly what the professor is asking of him or her and (2) done a good job of analyzing the policy concerns raised by the issue posed.

To do a good job on the first point, the key is taking your time. Read the question and think about it before answering. What precisely are you being asked about? Don't just write down the first thing that comes to mind.

To do a good job on the second point, don't worry about whether or not the professor will agree with the position you are taking. Focus instead on building a logical argument for whatever your position is using material covered in the course as much as possible.

E. MULTIPLE-CHOICE QUESTIONS

Increasingly, some Criminal Law professors use multiple-choice questions for all or part of their exams. To some extent, this may reflect the fact that the Multistate Bar Exam uses multiple-choice questions, and professors increasingly want to give their students experience prior to the Bar in answering those types of questions.

As with essay questions, multiple-choice Criminal Law questions can be quite different from one another. A common format is for the professor to set out a factual scenario, just like an issue-spotting exam, and then to ask a series of multiple-choice questions, each of which is based upon those same facts. In that format, typically the various questions deal with different issues and areas of the Criminal Law, all arising out of the same factual circumstances. In contrast, sometimes multiple-choice Criminal Law questions simply focus only upon a single area of Criminal Law.

This is an example of the latter format. Now, you can't really *answer* the question because you haven't finished your Criminal Law course! You have not studied the elements of a defense-of-property defense . . . *yet*. (And maybe, depending on what is covered in your particular course, you may not cover this subject at all.) Just as a matter of your continuing education, the correct answer to this multiple-choice question is (a).

Moreover, just like the issue-spotting example discussed previously, there are a handful of nonsubstantive things I can still point out to you taken from this example question that may be of use to you when you do begin to prepare for an examination like this later on. The comments in the margin refer to the places in the example question above where a number appears in superscript in square brackets.

AN EXAMPLE OF A CRIMINAL LAW MULTIPLE-CHOICE EXAM QUESTION

GRADER'S COMMENTS

Abel was asleep late one night when he heard a dragging noise outside his home that seemed to be coming from the front porch. He ran outside and saw Bennie carrying off a wicker rocker that he kept on the porch. Abel ran after Bennie, yelling, "Hey, put that back. That's my favorite chair!" Bennie kept running, but Abel quickly caught up with him and tackled him, causing Bennie to drop the chair. While Abel rescued his chair, he also injured Bennie in the process. As a result of being tackled, Bennie broke his left arm and his right wrist.[1]

Abel has been charged with the crime of assault on Bennie. Which of the following is most accurate:[2]

    (a) Abel has a valid defense of property defense in these circumstances.

    (b) Abel does not have a valid defense of property defense in these circumstances because that defense does not permit a person asserting it to physically assault someone.

    (c) Abel does not have a valid defense of property defense in these circumstances because the rocker was not affixed to his property.

    (d) Answers (b) and (c) are correct, but answer (a) is incorrect.[3]

1. Note that with this type of multiple-choice question, the fact pattern is relatively brief. Make sure you read the facts carefully. The correct answer often depends upon the way a single word or phrase has been used in the factual account or question.

2. This is an important part of the question. It doesn't ask you which answer is correct; instead, it asks which answer is *most* accurate. The implication, of course, is that some answers can be *more* correct than others. Those answers are the ones like answer (d) that, if accurate, include more than one correct answer to the question. (Of course, in this case, neither (b), (c), nor (d) was actually a correct answer. Only (a) was correct.)

3. Note that there are four possible answers here. If you had no idea what the correct answer was, a guess would give you a one in four chance of success. Do you want to take that risk? Well, before taking a multiple-choice exam, you need to find out whether your professor deducts points for wrong answers. If he or she does not, then—*hey!*—why not make your "best guess" about the correct answer? One in four times, you'll get an extra point. But, if you lose points for wrong answers, one in four is not good odds. You should see if you can eliminate a couple of the answer possibilities that appear clearly wrong. If you're going to guess, you really should wait until your odds are 50 percent or better.

CHAPTER 13

Final Thoughts

Hopefully, the preceding chapters have served as a useful introduction for you—a *jumpstart,* say—to help you approach, understand, and work with the substantive law that you will now be covering in your Criminal Law course.

  Criminal offenses and defenses.
  Guilt and innocence.
  Prosecution and defense.
  Trials and appeals.

As I noted at the very beginning of this book, all of these subjects arise and criminal proceedings take place in a larger context. The point of this *Jumpstart* exercise was both to explain and demystify that context for you and, importantly, to teach you some of the skills you need to understand (and perform) better in your Criminal Law course. And—*who knows?*—maybe this particular introduction and *Jumpstart* will even help you somewhere down the road in criminal defense or prosecution practice if that ends up to be part of your future career path.

When you begin to understand and appreciate the culture, the process, and the doctrine and the procedures of criminal justice adjudication, you are far better prepared to learn and to understand the substantive Criminal Law issues you will now be studying. At least, that's my sincere belief and hope. So . . . best of luck! Now that your (intellectual) engine has been *Jumpstarted . . . go to it!*

Index